HOME

ADELE BLAIR

NEW
HOLLAND

FOREWORD

"Adele's *HOME*, is truly a must-read book on organizing. It could just as easily be titled *Life's ABSOLUTE Instruction Book*. Her step-by-step approach to achieving order can and should be applied to all aspects of life… home, work, leisure and social. Adele explains how charting a course, making a plan of action and taking one step at a time will keep you on track to tackle any challenge. After reading this book you will exhale and say "ahhh". Thank you Adele for the roadmap to achieving serenity, even in our hectic lives!"

– Debbee Barker, Inventor of FlipFold, TV Personality and Organizational Expert

HOME

ACKNOWLEDGMENTS

Thank you to Anthony for being the most amazing partner
and for always believing in me.

Thanks to my Mum and Dad for showing me the value of hard work.

Thank you to my friends, colleagues, mentors and experts who supported me on this journey -
you all know who you are!

A special thanks to Cathy Player of Howards Storage World and to Diane Ward of New
Holland Publishing who turned an idea into reality.

A big hug to Dorothy Breninger for your friendship and contribution to this book.

CONTENTS

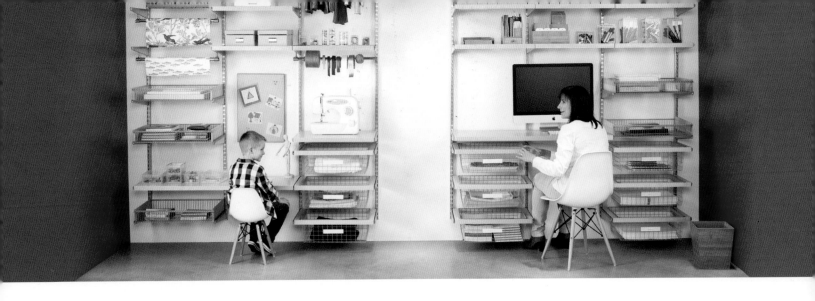

1

THE COST OF BEING DISORGANIZED

Most people believe that being disorganized is just 'the way it is' in today's busy world.

The truth is that it is more important than ever to create an organized environment for you and your family, because continuing to be disorganized can be costing you more than you think. In fact, some people don't believe that being disorganized has any impact on their life at all, it's just the way they operate... well think again.

Here are some sobering facts about what being disorganized is really costing you.

Cold Hard Cash
- How many times have you been hit with a late fee because you misplaced a bill?
- Have you had to pay extra interest on your credit card due to a late payment?
- Have you missed rebates from health insurance due to lost receipts?
- How many gift cards or gift vouchers have you been given and now can't find?
- What about coupons; do you collect them, but when you go to the stores, you realize that you have left them stuck to the fridge where they do you no good?

Lost Luxury
- How many times have you been given a gorgeous Day Spa voucher only to discover that it has expired by the time you find it to use?
- What about experience vouchers, such as hot air ballooning, or joy flights? Have you received one only to misplace it?
- Have you misplaced movie passes or a store voucher only to find it after it has expired?
- Have you missed out on special offers or two-for-one deals?

Late Again

- Have you had to pay late fees to your video store or library?
- Have you been charged a cancellation fee because you missed an appointment?
- What about when you are late to or missed a flight or didn't get your car out of the parking garage in time? These will almost certainly cost you money, not to mention stress!
- Have you been late to an important meeting because you hadn't organized the journey beforehand and got lost, i.e. you left without knowing the correct address, you didn't have your street directory in the car, or the navigator wasn't charged?

Time

- Think of the time you have lost looking for something you know you have, but you simply can't find it. This can result in more costs because you have to purchase a replacement item.
- Do you 'zig-zag' across town running errands because you haven't organized your trip properly. Again, this can add to costs just considering the price of gas, but it is also your wasted time?
- How many times do you have to run to the grocery store each week because you haven't planned your meals in advance? If you don't have time to get to the grocery store, you will probably end up eating take-out (see Health costs below).

Emotional

- Does it strain the relationship with your partner when you must repeatedly pay unnecessary late fees?
- Have you ever had a 'tiff' with a friend because they have loaned you a treasured item and when they ask you for it, you are unable to find it?
- Do you feel embarrassed about the state of your home should you have drop-in guests?
- Do you ever feel fatigued, stressed, or simply overwhelmed when you think about your current state of organization?

Professional

- Some people can work perfectly in a disorganized environment, but from the outside, it can present the impression that you are incapable of managing tasks, and your lack of organization could potentially be a CLM (Career Limiting Move).
- Do you think a disorganized work environment can make you look unprofessional?

- Have you been overlooked for a special assignment or project because your boss thinks you can't handle extra work?
- If you are a manager, does your work area create the right example for your sub-ordinates?

Personal

- Are you a Mrs. Messy married to Mr. Tidy, or the reverse?
- Are you consistently late when catching up with friends? If constantly repeated, this can make your friends feel second rate, as though whatever was making you late was more important than them.
- Have you been embarrassingly late for a meeting because you hadn't planned what to wear (you had no fresh pantyhose, only dirty shoes, or a button missing from your blouse/shirt)?
- Are you 'short tempered' with your family because you are always disorganized?
- Do you miss out on spending precious time with your family because you're too busy chasing your tail?

Health

- Regardless of the emotional costs, what about your health? Is clutter in your home causing allergies?
- Are you having anxiety attacks because you can't have friends over for dinner?
- Do you have so much clutter that you can't get into your bed for a good nights' rest? Your bedroom should be a place of sanctuary and rest.
- Do you end up having take-out often because you are never organized enough to go to the store to buy healthy food for your family?

As you can see, there are many ways that being disorganized can affect your life and the lives of your family, friends and work colleagues. I am sure that you can think of other ways being disorganized has cost you.

2

OVERCOMING EXCUSES

Do you have a million reasons (read: excuses) for why you can't get organized?
Do you feel defeated before you even get started? Believe me, we have all been where
you are. Everyone uses the same excuses to avoid getting things organized.
For every excuse you can find to use, there is a solution.

"There's just too much stuff!"

The way out of feeling overwhelmed by stuff is to reduce the amount of it. If there is just too much stuff, it's time to remove some. Whether you donate it, hold a garage sale, advertise on online auction sites, or just throw it away – the goal is to reduce the amount of stuff.

"I don't know where to start"

Just pick a place to start and go for it. The purpose of this book is to help you look at organizing as a series of small projects. When you have identified an organizing project, turn to that chapter and follow the steps.

"I don't have time"

If getting organized is important to you then schedule it into your calendar. Never wait for some 'spare time' before undertaking an organizing project because it just won't happen. Like anything important, such as a holiday or a party, you schedule time for it in your planner for a specific day at a specific time. Treat your organizing projects the same way.

"I want to get it all done now"

Lower your expectations. It took you longer than overnight to get where you are now and making it go away won't happen overnight either. Be realistic. Set a time or plan a schedule and take one step at a time. Like the age-old saying, "How do you eat an elephant? One bite at a time!" The same thing applies to a large organizing project.

"I don't know how to go about getting organized"

Well, you have made the best start by reading this book. There are also many other online resources to help you. If you need the support of a professional, find a Professional Organizer at NAPO (National Association for Professional Organizers) or AAPO (Australian Association of Professional Organizers).

"My spouse won't toss anything"

So, start somewhere else and don't worry about your spouse's belongings just yet. You may get a surprise when you start achieving organizing success in other parts of your home, the rest of the family may just get on board!

"I get it organized, but it doesn't stay that way"

…And it won't unless you put routines in place to help you maintain it. It is much the same as maintaining a weight loss program; you have to consistently monitor your calorie intake and exercise regime. Once you achieve your weight loss goal, you won't maintain that weight if you return to your old habits. Likewise, establishing routines ensure that you maintain new, beneficial organizing habits.

"My children undo whatever I do"

No matter what age your children are, they can have responsibilities around the home. Hold a family meeting and discuss all of the things that need to happen to keep your home running smoothly. Let your children choose which age-appropriate chores to do. If they choose them, they are more likely to complete them. Let them know that they can re-negotiate which chores they prefer at the next meeting.

Remember, you are the parent; you are in charge. Teach them what they need to know to be a functioning, responsible adult.

"But, I might need it someday"

The reality is that you won't miss much of anything that you part with at all. In fact, you may not even remember that you've tossed it. The goal right now is to clear the clutter and regain your life. The value of creating an organized and functioning family home is far greater than potentially having to replace an item that you may have gotten rid of in the process.

"I don't know what I should get rid of"

In Chapter 4, The Basics of Decluttering, I show you some sorting methods and how to know what to get rid of. In short, there are two simple questions to ask yourself when making that decision:

1. *Do I absolutely love it?*
2. *Do I use it – regularly?*

If you answer yes to both questions, that item should be retained. If not the item should be thrown away, donated or sold. Refer to our chapter on How to Organize a Garage/Yard Sale if you like the idea of cashing in on your organizing efforts.

3

AN INTRODUCTION TO ORGANIZING

Getting organized enables you to create a clear space in which to focus on systems and strategies that suit your personal lifestyle. Before you call for a dumpster, pull out the garbage bags, and call your girlfriend to help, take a moment to consider what organizing is.

First, let's be clear about what organizing is not. Organizing is not about being orderly, tidy, minimalistic, or having your home looking like an advertisement in a glossy home magazine.

Interestingly enough, your home can look like it has been lifted from the pages of a magazine, but what happens when someone opens a cupboard? Or, how about when you are asked to retrieve something you know you have, but you just can't quite put your hand on it? Things don't feel quite so organized then, do they?

The basis of being organized is:
- Creating a system of retrieval that suits your lifestyle, thus saving you loads of time;
- Making sure your belongings are equal to or less than the space you have to store them; and
- Ensuring that your environment is functional and suits your family, rather than just looking tidy.

Research recently undertaken by the Australian Institute revealed that there are four key types of clutter: Emotional, Just-In-Case, Fad and Bargain Clutter.

Understanding what type of 'clutterer' you are can be very helpful in your quest to becoming more organized.

Attachment to Stuff

Excessive amounts of stuff or clutter accumulates from an assortment of items, which may be extremely varied depending on the circumstances and personalities within each household. These items can generally be placed into four categories of clutter depending on the nature of your attachment to the stuff, for example:

Emotional Clutter

Emotional Clutter is comprised of things that have sentimental meaning but little financial value. They include children's toys, drawings, (unused or unwanted) gifts, school or university notes, the personal possessions of an absent loved one, and many other things that we hold onto purely for their sentimental value.

With emotional clutter, it is important to ask yourself if you are truly honoring and cherishing this item and the memories it represents. If it is sitting under a pile of clutter or in a dusty box, what value are you really placing on it?

If you simply must keep it but you don't have the space or a proper place to put it, try one of these ideas:

- Take photos of precious memories and create a scrapbook or memory book. Remember that the mementos are not the memories; the memories may come to mind when you view the mementos, but sometimes you just need to see the item (or even a photo of it) to re-live those memories.
- Create a memory box for special people in your life, and limit your collection to the capacity of that box.
- Scan or take photos of the children's school paintings and save them to a disk. You can use the images as a screensaver or to create a photo book. Remember that, over time, the children's artwork and craft items will deteriorate and may be munched away by insects, so this option is a great way to ensure that doesn't happen. Saved to a disk, they will keep forever, so you can pass them on to your children.
- Just because something was a gift doesn't mean you have to keep it. If it is in good condition but simply doesn't suit your lifestyle, consider giving it to another family member (particularly if it is a family treasure), or selling it and buying something more meaningful.

The key to dealing with emotional clutter is ensuring that the way you treat the item truly reflects the value you claim it has.

Just-In-Case Clutter

Just-in-case clutter consists of things that have little or no sentimental value that we keep because they 'might come in handy one day'. We often hold on to these things for quite some time after they are no longer useful to us. They might be old bills or bank statements, tools or stationery

Sometimes, holding onto too much stuff that we may "possibly" use in the future can prevent us from living in the present. Being prepared for the future is a good thing, but not when it takes over your life in the present day.

Have you ever had a situation where you find it difficult to give up an item because it seems useful so you keep it 'just in case'? Next time, ask yourself, what is the likelihood of that happening? It is probably very unlikely that you need to use 25 same-sized plastic containers at exactly the same time, or that you need to have 12 sets of towels when there are only two people living in your home.

This is the time for a bit of a reality check about whether the 'just in case' situation you are keeping the item for will really ever happen. Old bills only need to be kept for about 18 months or, if that bill has been included as part of a taxation claim, it should be retained in accordance with your state's Statute of Limitations for audits.

An oversupply of stationery and office supplies is very common; gorgeous papers and paperclips can seduce us all. Unless you have a full-scale office, you don't need to keep a huge supply of these items.

If you want to get rid of it, consider offering it to a charity (they do not only need clothes. They also need stationery to run their administration), or to your local pre-school or church.

Fad Clutter

Fad Clutter accumulates from impulse purchases, often acquired recently, that never end up being used. They commonly include clothes, fashion accessories or books.

We can all be a little guilty of this. We see the latest fashion trend and simply must have it, but we wear it once and, quick as a flash, it is out of style.

Similarly, with technology, as soon as manufacturers release the latest model or a new device, we quickly set aside the old version in preference of the new.

So, the question is; what to do with those items? You paid good money for them, but you don't use them anymore because they have been superseded by something else.

A simple solution is to give it to charity, a friend, or a family member. Another alternative is to sell it through an online auction site or hold a garage sale. Selling these types of items not only generates money you didn't have before, it also reduces your Fad Clutter.

HOME HINT: *Fad Clutter and fashion—if you are holding onto designer clothes in the hope that you will wear it again when it comes back into vogue, here's a tip: you won't!*

Whenever fashions do re-appear they are never exactly the same as before; there is always a new cut, color, fabric or style variation.

Also, if you wore it the first time around, then you probably should reconsider wearing it the second.

I am having a flashback to high-waisted jeans that were fashionable in the 80s. I couldn't possibly bring myself to wear them again now – I'm not 19 anymore!

Bargain Clutter

Bargain Clutter is comprised of things that are free, or very cheap; items we acquire at sales, from friends or family, or 'by the side of the road'. We discard them only reluctantly because they were so cheap.

Confession time: this describes me! I absolutely love a bargain and often shock my friends at the bargains I can snare.

Now, I am not saying that your bargain-shopping days are over; however, what I would suggest is that you don't buy something simply because it is cheap. A good prompt is to ask yourself: Would you buy it if it were full retail price? If the answer is yes, then this is something you are buying for the right reasons.

So, how do you deal with these items? Perhaps you could give it away to charity, a friend, or a family member. Alternatively, you could sell it and earn some money from your bargains.

4

THE BASICS OF DECLUTTERING

Sometimes you just don't know what to do with things you don't really need.
You may think things like "Is it wasteful if I throw it away? What else can I do with it?
Maybe I should just keep it after all." When you are ready to de-clutter, you start
wondering, "What do I keep? What do I throw? How do I decide?"

Quite often, we start a de-clutter project with plenty of enthusiasm; we lay out tubs, set aside the whole day on the calendar, and even make a sandwich for lunch and get off to a flying start!

Then comes the time when the actual sorting needs to begin, but, instead, you find yourself at a standstill, not knowing where to start.

This is one of the main reasons de-clutter projects never get finished; because we simply don't know how to sort or what to do with all the stuff. It can be very overwhelming. You may get through a few cupboards and boxes easily. Then, you run out of motivation because you have struck a problem – "what do I do with this?"

Sorting

You may wonder why you should bother sorting stuff out. After all, it seems easier to just toss things into 'keep and throw' piles, right?

Well, in theory that might sound OK, but you need to factor in other things, such as items you might want to give to charity, items that you need to return to friends, items that need to be stored in another area of the house, and of course, those items you want to keep.

Sorting into categories is essential if you want to avoid ending up with two piles that seem even more overwhelming than the original clutter did.

Sorting starts to bring some kind of sense to your clutter and really cuts down on your workload toward the end of the project. While it can be easier to simply stop the sorting process when it becomes too difficult, remember your goals and why you are undertaking the project. That's what is most important – it's not just about the stuff.

I have used a number of different sorting methods to help clients work through these stumbling blocks.

HOME HINT: *Don't waste time; this is not the time to reminisce over photos or mementos.*

Handle each item once and don't put it down until you have made your decision ("I don't know" is not a decision).

How much stuff is going into the trash pile? This should be the fastest growing pile when doing a sort. The bigger the trash pile, the less work for you later on.

Don't stop until you are finished, and when you are, move all the items for trash or donation out of the house immediately. You can put the donation items straight into the trunk of your car.

If you are working with family members and you can't decide jointly what to do with a particular item, don't argue about it now; set it to one side to discuss calmly later on.

Sorting Methods

There are many different sorting methods; this section by no means includes all of them. These ideas are intended to inspire you to get creative and find a way that works for you and help you reach your sorting goals.

The methods I have included here are those that have been most successful with our clients. Each of the sorting methods described may hold more or less appeal for you based on your personality and the relationship you have with your clutter.

A Professional Organizer, if you choose to hire one to help you with your de-clutter project, may well have a different method entirely. Try anything and everything until you find something that works; don't give up!

It really doesn't matter which method you use, as long as you get the results you want and reach the goal you have set for yourself.

Finally, once you have found a sorting method that works for you, stick to it. Don't change methods half way through if you can help it. Read on and you'll see what I mean.

Traditional Sorting Method

This is the traditional, or shall I say basic style of sorting. Lay out tubs and label as follows: Staying – This Room, Staying – Other Room, Donate, Give/Return to a Friend.

What do they mean?

- 'Staying – This Room' – is for all items that fit within the function, feel and look of the room and must be kept.
- 'Staying – Other Room' – all items that you need to keep but that don't belong in this room.
- 'Donate' – are items that you would like to give to charity.
- 'Give/Return to a Friend' – items that you would prefer to give to a friend or family member, or ones you have borrowed and need to return to them.

Label tubs, for example Keep, Rubbish or Donate

HOME HINT: *Take breaks of no more than 10 minutes. Otherwise, you risk becoming distracted, losing focus, and stopping the project. Avoid leaving the room when possible; turn off the phone, and arrange to have the kids stay with friends or a babysitter.*

Step 1   Use plastic garbage bags to throw away any trash/items so you can put them straight into the trash when full.

Step 2   Start at the entrance and work your way around the room in one direction.

Step 3 Once all the tubs are full and your room is empty with the exception of the very large pieces of furniture, it is time to give it a cleaning.

Step 4 Deal with the tubs that are not returning to the space. Put the 'Give to a Friend' tub and the 'Donate' tub in your car immediately. Put the 'Staying – Other Room' tub(s) in another room ready for when you commence that organizing project.

Step 5 Put the trash in the bin immediately. If you have more trash than you anticipated, consider hiring a specialized rubbish removal service.

HOME HINT: *If you find items that you want to keep but they need repairing, consider if the item is really worth repairing from a cost perspective. Once you have the item repaired, do you realistically think you will use it?*

The Yesterday, Today and Tomorrow Method

We know this is the name of a gorgeous shrub, but it is also the name of our next method of sorting. Lay out three tubs and label them as follows: 'Yesterday', 'Today' and 'Tomorrow'.

What do they mean?
- 'Yesterday' – is for all items that were relevant to your past life, but no longer have a place in your life now. The 'Yesterday' tub can also be the garbage bin and/or the donate bin!
- 'Today' – for all items that you need to keep because they are essential to your life today, right now, in the present. These are things that you use every day or at least every week.
- 'Tomorrow' – are items that you would like to keep and, most importantly, will use in the future.

Step 1 Use plastic garbage bags for any trash/items to throw away so you can put them straight into the trash bin when full.

Step 2 Start at the entrance, and work your way around the room in one direction.

Step 3 Pick up each item and ask yourself if it belongs in your past life (Yesterday), if it belongs and will enhance your life in the present (Today), or if perhaps, you should hang onto it for the future (Tomorrow).

Step 4   Remove all the contents of the Yesterday tub and re-sort them into items to donate or give away to friends or family or trash.

Step 5   Put the trash in the garbage can immediately. If you have more trash than you anticipated, consider hiring a specialized rubbish removal service.

HOME HINT: *Be careful when deciding to place an item in the 'Tomorrow' tub. Make sure that you are not overloading it with 'Just-In-Case' items.*

The Strangers, Acquaintances and Friends Method

The title of this method sounds a bit strange, doesn't it? However, this method is fantastic for people who really treat their belongings like friends or 'people'.

As with real-life friends, clutter may actually fall into other categories such as strangers or simple acquaintances.

Read on to see how this one works.

Lay out three tubs and label as follows: Strangers, Acquaintances and Friends.

What do they mean?

- 'Strangers' – is for all those items you hardly ever use, see, or are really that bothered about. These items really are strangers; your life has gone on perfectly well without them.
- 'Acquaintances' – is for all the items that you don't see often but quite enjoy their company (or use) when you do.
- 'Friends' – is for the items that you really cherish, just like a true friend. These items are always useful, helpful and required to help you in everyday life. They can also be special items given to you by important people in your life.

Step 1   Use plastic garbage bags for any trash / items to throw away so you can put them straight into the trash bin when it's full.

Step 2   Start at the entrance of the room and work your way around the space in one direction.

Step 3   Pick up each item and ask yourself if it really is a complete stranger; you haven't seen it for weeks, months, years and haven't really missed it. If the answer is 'yes', then it belongs in the 'Strangers' tub (as well as trash). If you need the item sometimes, put it in your 'Acquaintances' tub. If it is a loved, honored, and often used item, then pop it into your 'Friends' tub.

Step 4   Once all the tubs are full and your room is empty with the exception of the very large pieces of furniture, now is the time to give it a cleaning.

Step 5   Remove all the contents of the 'Strangers' tub and re-sort them into items to donate or give away to friends or family, the remainder should be considered trash.

Step 6   Put the trash in the bin immediately. If you have more trash than you anticipated, consider hiring a specialized rubbish removal service.

Step 7   Review your 'Acquaintance' tub. This will be the most difficult to sort as you need to really decide if they should be kept or thrown – how much do you need the item, will it enhance your life, should it become a true friend?

Step 8   The same applies for your 'Friends' tub. Make sure that these friends really do have a positive effect on your life. For example, you may absolutely love a blouse you have, you spent a lot of money on it and it is truly gorgeous, but you never feel quite right when you wear it. Perhaps you don't actually wear it for that reason? Give these toxic friends a bit of a rethink!

HOME HINT: *Beware of toxic friends! You may have heard this term when talking about people who say they are friends but who actually make you feel terrible when you spend time with them; they bring you down and are negative all the time. Belongings can give you the same feeling and are not true friends.*

The Plan a Party Method

Sounds a bit strange, doesn't it? This method is similar to the Strangers, Acquaintances, and Friends method. The main difference is that it is a little more decisive.

Lay out two tubs and label as follows: 'Yes' and 'No'.

What do they mean?

- 'Yes' – is for all the items you would definitely invite to a party. You love them, love their company, they make you feel good, they are really useful, they lend a helping hand, and are an all-round good thing to have nearby.
- 'No' – are items that are really boring, never have anything positive or happy to say, never add any real value to your life, and you really wonder why you ever had them on your invitation list to start with!

Step 1   Use plastic garbage bags for any trash/items to throw away; all of these items are definitely not invited to the party!

Step 2   Start at the entrance and work your way around the room in one direction.

Step 3   Pick up each item and ask yourself if they are on the party list or not? I did say this method was very decisive; the item either adds an enormous amount of positive value to your life now or it simply doesn't. There is no in between!

Step 4   Take breaks of no more than 10 minutes; otherwise, you risk becoming distracted, losing focus, and stopping the project. Avoid leaving the room when possible, turn off the phone, and arrange to have the kids be with friends or a babysitter.

Step 5   Once all the tubs are full and your room is empty, with the exception of the very large pieces of furniture, now is the time to give it a cleaning.

Step 6   Remove all the contents of the 'No' tub and re-sort them into items to donate or give away to friends or family, the remainder should be considered trash.

Step 7   Put the trash in the bin immediately. If you have more trash than you anticipated, consider hiring a specialized rubbish removal service.

The Treasure Hunt Method

Who would have thought that de-cluttering could involve a treasure hunt? This method is particularly good for those of you who are super-overwhelmed.

Lay out two tubs and label as follows: 'Hunted' and 'Gathered'.

What do they mean?
- 'Hunted' – treasures you have hunted down in the space you are de-cluttering and you absolutely have to keep.
- 'Gathered' – are items that are left behind.

Step 1   Start anywhere in the room, and set an egg timer for 10 minutes.

Step 2   Commence the Treasure Hunt with your timer and select the treasures or your 'Hunted' items. Your instinct will tell you which items to select.

Step 3 Pick up 10 items (within the 10 minutes), that you consider to be 'Treasure' and put them in your 'Hunted' tub. These are things that you absolutely cannot live without; they are essential to your day-to-day life and you love them.

Step 4 Repeat no more than 4 or 5 times.

Step 5 Start the timer again, this time you are 'Gathering'.

Step 6 These are the items that are less important to you. These are items that you need to decide about whether to donate, throw away or give to friends or family.

HOME HINT: *Do not simply continue putting the timer on until you have collected ALL your items as treasure. This method is designed to help your instinct take over and tell you what is really important.*

Step 7 Once all the tubs are full and your room is empty with the exception of the very large pieces of furniture, now is the time to give it a cleaning.

Step 8 For items that have been 'Hunted', these can be returned to their correct location (or re-organized into like-with-like groups and stored accordingly).

Step 9 Remove all the contents of the 'Gathered' tub and re-sort them into items to donate or give away to friends or family, the remainder should be considered trash.

Step 10 Put the trash in the bin immediately. If you have more trash than you anticipated, consider hiring a specialized rubbish removal service.

HOME HINT: *A great place to try the Treasure Hunt method is a knick-knack or display cabinet, where there are many treasures, but you can only keep a few (remember, you are de-cluttering, after all).*

Step 11 For items that are to be donated or given away, put them immediately into your car so they can be delivered sooner rather than later.

Congratulations! You have worked your way through most of your clutter, but now you are really stuck. You have a few things left over that you really don't know what to do with.

If the item logically belongs in another space within your home, return it to that space (for example tools should be returned to the garage or garden shed).

If you have further items that you want to keep but simply don't know what to do with, I would recommend that you pack them away into a storage tub. Put a note in your planner to revisit that tub in six months and review the items again. You may have thought the item was very important during the declutter, but when you review it a second time, its importance may have diminished, making it easier to make a decision.

Summary of Sorting

As I mentioned at the beginning of this chapter, there are many methods of sorting that can help you get through the clutter. The main goal, as Peter Wash says, "It's not about the stuff, it is about your relationship with the stuff and how you deal with it."

If your clutter is causing you to feel overwhelmed, anxious, stressed and generally blah, you have definitely made the right choice for you and your family to do something about it.

I know that one method of sorting does not suit everyone, so I hope I have provided you with some inspiration that will help you work through your clutter.

HOME HINT: *When considering items for donation, remember that, while people need charity, they still have dignity. Make sure that all donated items are in good, clean condition. A good rule of thumb is that if you wouldn't ask a friend to pay you $5 for it then it's not worth donating.*

5

HOW TO ORGANIZE MY KITCHEN

Ainsley has bought an amazing beachside bungalow, but along with this amazing location comes a very tired kitchen. She and her husband plan on living in the house for a year or two before making any renovations. Unfortunately that means living with a new-born (she is 5 months pregnant) in a kitchen dating from the 1940s. I need to get it organized before the baby arrives!

This project will happen in five stages:

Stage 1 – Evaluate your Space/Zones

Step 1   Make room on the calendar for 1–2 hours for this stage.

Step 2   Grab your supplies:
- Notepad
- Pen

Step 3   Sit down in your kitchen and think about the activities that happen in this area. For example, food preparation, home office, kids doing homework and so on. List these down on your notepad.

Step 4   Evaluate your space and see if you realistically have enough designated zones (areas) to undertake these activities. If you do not, you may need to re-evaluate and consider moving some of those activities to another area within your home (space permitting). Prioritize activities in order of the ones that are most important within the kitchen area.

Step 5 Once you have designated zones for your activities, think about what these zones may need to really make them 'work' and write a list of supplies (this will obviously depend on your budget, if yzou have one). For example, you may need additional storage, more lighting, shelving units, telephone/data points, and so on.

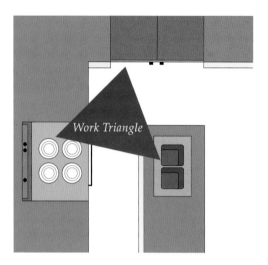

HOME HINT: *Kitchens should ultimately have a triangular layout between the sink, stove and refrigerator, as shown in this diagram. This is a great starting point for organizing your zones.*

Stage 2 – Clear the Pantry

Step 1 Gather your supplies:
- Garbage bags
- Large boxes or tubs
- New storage containers you may have purchased
- Cleaning products

Step 2 Do a quick sort through your pantry and throw away any items that are beyond their Use By or Best Before Date (refer to How to Organize My Pantry if you feel your pantry needs extra attention).

HOME HINT: *Why sort the pantry now? Often a pantry can be crammed full of out of date or unused items that are taking up valuable storage space that may come in handy in the next stages.*

Step 3   Evaluate the items that remain in your pantry that are not in a container; opened packets of food stuffs take up much more space than containers.

Check out what suitable containers you may already have that you could utilize in the pantry.

If you do not have any, then add them to the list of items you may need to purchase. Here are our suggestions for the average pantry.

- 4 x 5 liter containers (for flours, pasta, sugar)
- 8 x 2.5 liter containers (for rice, breadcrumbs, lentils)
- 6 x 1.5 liter containers (for cous cous, cornstarch)
- 4 x 0.5 liter containers (for cocoa, sprinkles)

HOME HINT: *Always use square or rectangular containers in your pantry as they take up less space than circular containers do.*

Step 4   Review other items that you store in your pantry, for example electrical appliances or storage containers.

Stage 3 – Decluttering the Space

Step 1   Make sure you have a large, clear space available nearby, the dining room table, for example.

Step 2   Gather your supplies:
- Garbage bags
- Large boxes or tubs
- New storage containers you may have purchased
- Cleaning products

Step 3   Empty all the contents of your kitchen (excluding the pantry) onto the dining room table or whatever work space you have created.

Depending on the size of the space you have, you may need to do Steps 4, 5 and 6 a couple of times, working through different areas in the kitchen.

Step 4 Sort through all of the contents deciding what items can be thrown, donated, or kept and place them into the appropriate tubs/boxes. If you are unsure, create an 'unsure' box and keep those items there for the time being.

Step 5 Be ruthless with your de-cluttering, if you have loads of gadgets that were a good idea at the time, but you have never used them, get rid of them.

Consider how many saucepans you have. If you have over ten and you do not do much cooking, consider donating some of them. If you have loads of baking tins and trays but rarely bake, review their usefulness also.

Match all plastic lids and bottoms. Throw away those that do not have partners and ones that have warped through over-use in the dishwasher.

If something needs repair, you need to consider if it is worth it. Often, it may be easier to replace it, particularly electrical items.

Cooking Zone

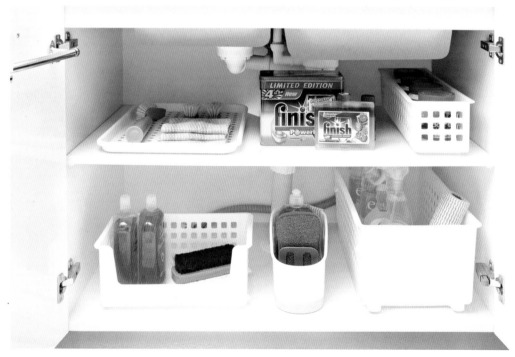

Cleaning Zone

HOME HINT: *Some charities may not accept broken electrical items, as they simply do not have the funds to repair them, and of course, there are safety concerns about second hand appliances. Call ahead and check first.*

Step 6   Clean all the drawers and cupboards, giving them a good scrub. If you have some badly stained shelves, consider covering them with white contact paper. This will give them a much needed freshening up.

Stage 4 – Organize the Zones

Step 1   After clearly deciding on the items you wish to retain, those that are being donated or those to be thrown away, return the items to be kept to the correct zones that you created in Stage 1.

   If you have a budget for your kitchen organizing project, you might want to think about hiring an electrician to add or move power points or more lighting if that would help when re-organizing your zones.

Step 2   Return your 'keep' items to the kitchen, making sure to place them in their new zones. If you are still unsure where items should go, some simple hints are:
   • Keep items next to where they are most used, for example saucepans next to the stove, glassware next to the fridge.
   • Store all like items together, i.e. all glassware, cutlery, utensils, etc.
   • Remove all 'non-kitchen' items to another, more appropriate place within the home. For example household tools often end up in the kitchen, consider moving them to the garage or the laundry room. Stationery items and office supplies can overtake an entire drawer; consider moving them to a home office area.

Step 3   Are you running short of storage space within your newly created zones? At the end of this chapter, we have included some space-creating ideas that you might like to try.

HOME HINT: *Do you have too many things permanently living on your counter tops (the toaster, canisters, TV, or a blender)? Limit the items on the counter to those you use every day. Store the others out of the way in cabinets or on pantry shelves.*

Stage 5 – The Refrigerator

Step 1   Empty the contents of your refrigerator onto your workspace. Throw away any food that is beyond its Best Before or Use By date.

Step 2   Wipe out the fridge using warm water with a little Baking Soda.

Step 3   Return the items to the refrigerator again using the like-with-like method. For example, you may choose to put all your jams, jellies and spreads on a door shelf, all the drinks on the bottom shelf, etc.

HOME HINT: *To keep your sauces and condiments neatly together in your fridge, place them all into a plastic basket or tray. These are readily available and a variety of homemaker stores including Howards Storage World. Then, when you need to use them, lift the entire tray out of the fridge, select the item you need then pop the tray back. This saves anything from getting lost at the back of the fridge.*

Enjoy! You will need to 'road-test' your newly created zones for a few weeks to make sure they actually work. If they don't, just tweak them until you feel comfortable with them.

6

HOW TO ORGANIZE MY PANTRY

Annie has an amazing kitchen, but she has been unable to make the most of her pantry.
She has a mix of different containers, some food packets are sealed with elastic bands
or clothespins and she can't find things that she needs. She has a number of
wonderful containers but they remain in their wrapping, unused.
I need to help her get the most from her space.

Step 1   Schedule a couple of hours for this one. Yes, I know it sounds like a long time to spend on such a small area, but believe me, organizing a pantry can be very time consuming.

Step 2   Gather your supplies:
- Garbage bags
- Large boxes or tubs
- New storage containers you may have purchased
- Cleaning products

Step 3   Make sure that your kitchen counter and sink is absolutely clear and clean.

Step 4   Take out all the items from only one shelf of your pantry and put them on the counter. Focusing on one shelf at a time keeps you from overloading your counter or workspace.

HOME HINT: *Schedule your pantry project for the day before the trash collection so you can get rid of any expired foodstuffs immediately.*

Step 5   Check the Best Before or Use By date on each item and dispose of anything that is out of date. Also, throw away anything that has been unsealed for any length of time; it has more than likely spoiled.

Step 6   Put all the items you wish to keep to one side and repeat Steps 3 and 4 for the remaining shelves in your pantry.

You should now have all your out of date items in the trash, and everything on your counter is good to keep – right?

Step 7   Putting all of your opened items in containers is definitely the way to go to ensure an organized pantry. Now is the time to make use of all of your plastic, air-tight containers to store these items so that they stay fresh.

Step 8   Label your containers. If you don't have labels or a label maker and you don't want to write on your containers, cut a piece of the packaging that states what product it is

from and place it inside the container. This is especially useful when trying to identify thing such as plain flour from self-rising flour, or salt from sugar!

HOME HINT: *If you have containers that need washing (grubby finger marks or food stains), empty the contents into a bowl and give the container a quick clean before filling it back up.*

Step 9 Wipe down all the shelves in your pantry. To give your pantry a lovely, fresh smell, add a couple drops of Orange Essential Oil to your cloth and wipe it over the shelves. Your pantry will smell so fresh and clean.

Step 10 Put all your items into groups on the counter. For example baking items (flours, cocoa and sugars etc) belong together, as do all your dry goods (rice, couscous, lentils and pastas), general pantry goods (cereals, biscuits, savoury snacks), canned foods and so on.

Step 11 Return the items to the pantry putting the most frequently used items on the shelf at elbow level. If you are like my family we would put breakfast cereals, chips, bread items, spreads etc on this shelf. The next most frequently used should go on the shelf above, and finally, place the least used items on the top shelf.

Step 12 If your pantry is very deep or has tall shelves, maximise the space by either stacking your containers on top of each other or investing in some racks to help you utilize the space more efficiently.

HOME HINT: *Place items with the soonest Use By date or Best Before date toward the front so they are used first.*

Step 13 Put a reminder in your calendar or planner to do this every six months and your pantry will always be organized! If you don't want this to be a huge job every six months, it takes just a couple of seconds to put items back into your pantry correctly after each use.

7

HOW TO ORGANIZE MY RECIPES

While organizing Liz's home office, I found many recipes that were clipped from magazines or written on notes from friends. She then informed me that she also has many recipes that friends had emailed to her after dinner parties. It frustrates her that each time she remembers a fantastic recipe that she saw 'somewhere', she can never find it. I need to show her a simple system that will work.

Step 1   Schedule at least an hour to complete this task. Clear some space to work in; the dining room table is ideal.

Step 2   Gather your supplies:
- A three-ring binder
- A set of at least ten tabs (get the extra wide ones)
- Clear plastic sleeves (page protectors)
- Scissors
- Access to a photocopier (optional)

Step 3   Gather all those random recipes you have scattered around the house or office. These include pages torn out of magazines, recipes from friends – anything you can find that has a recipe on it that you wish to try, or that you have already tried and love.

Step 4   After ensuring your dining room table (or other work space) is completely clear, start laying out the recipes in groups. These are my suggested groups/categories:

- Chicken
- Beef
- Fish
- Lamb
- Pork
- Game
- Savory
- Vegetables/Vegetarian
- Pasta/Rice
- Slices/Cakes
- Desserts
- Other

If your recipes don't fit these categories, simply create any categories that suit your taste and lifestyle.

HOME HINT: *If your recipe is still secured in a magazine, consider photocopying the recipe instead of ripping it out. You can then recycle the magazine by passing it onto a friend, donating it to a doctor's office or clinic, church group, or even a playgroup (great for cut and paste).*

Step 5   Once you have sorted the recipes into categories, check how many duplicate recipes you have. Do you really need three recipes for Macaroni and Cheese? Are they all the same? Can you perhaps get rid of one? Is there a recipe that you have tried and didn't like? This is the step where you 'fine tune' the recipes you have selected, being sure to only include the ones you really want.

Step 6   Determine whether you need to create any additional categories. For example, you might want to make one for Kids Favorites or School Snacks/Lunches or Picnic Foods, etc.

HOME HINT: *What about all your favorite recipes in your cookbooks? Photocopy your favorites and insert them into your categories; or make a note of the recipe on a piece of paper with the reference to the cookbook and insert it into the relevant category.*

Step 7   By this stage you should have your favorite recipes (tried or not) sorted into categories. On your tabs, write down the categories you have made.

Step 8 Insert the recipes back-to-back in the clear plastic sleeves.

HOME HINT: *Consider creating a second file with those recipes that you don't use every day. You could create categories for:*

- Dinner Parties
- Kids Birthdays
- Christmas

- Picnic Food
- How To (i.e. cooking methods)
- Condiments (jams, chutneys, sauces, etc.)

Step 9 File all your plastic sleeves behind the relevant tabs and place them into your three-ring binder.

Step 10 Store your binder in an easily accessible shelf in your kitchen so it is quick and handy to use. Sometimes, the nice little space beside the microwave is just right.

Step 11 When you add new recipes to your binder, take a quick look at the recipes you have yet to try. If some recipes no longer appeal, simply remove them. This will keep your custom recipe book perfectly up to date.

HOME HINT: *If you try a recipe from your folder that you don't like, simply pull it out and throw it away. No point keeping recipes for meals you don't enjoy!*

A great feature of this system is, each time you find a recipe that you like you can tear it out, photocopy or print it, and file it away immediately. No more recipes lying around or, worse still, getting lost forever.

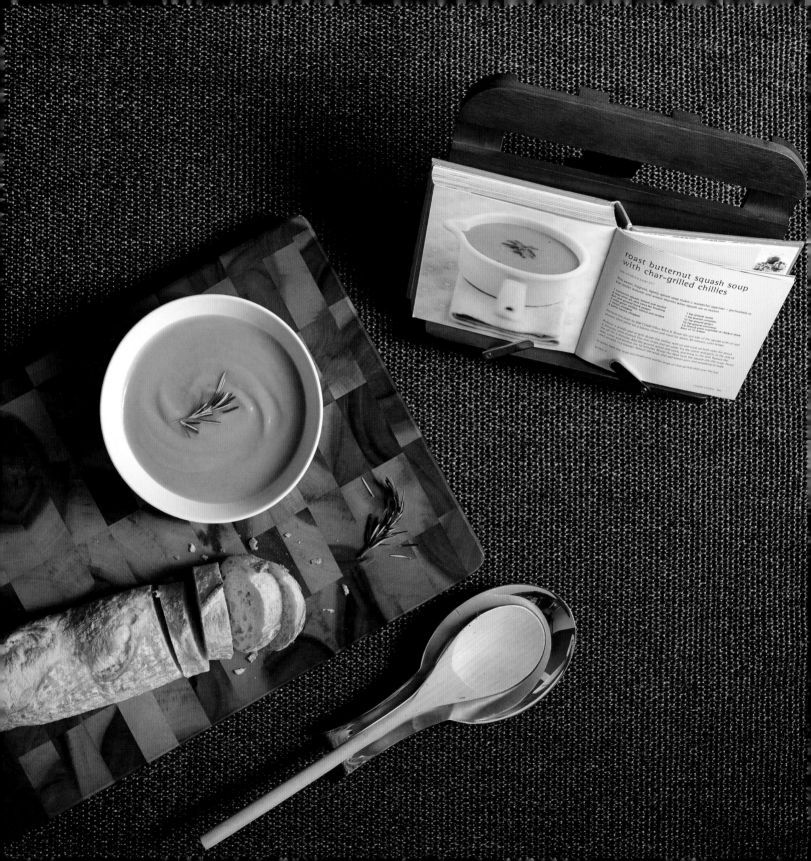

roast butternut squash soup with char-grilled chillies

8

HOW TO ORGANIZE MY MEALS

Suzie has two children. She and her husband both work full time, and they are on a budget. Not only are they on a money budget, they are on a calorie budget as well. My focus here is to have Suzie's meals organized ahead of meal times to help her save time and money while providing healthy meals for her family.

Step 1 Now that you have organized your recipes (see previous chapter) you should have a good idea of what you and your family like to eat.

Step 2 Lets create a menu plan for the next week. Grab a pen and pad or if you have one, a menu planning notepad, these are available at most stationers

Step 3 When planning your meals for the next seven days, consider the items that you already have in the fridge, especially any that are due to expire soon. Start your meal planning with ones that use those items. Doing this saves time spent shopping and avoids waste.

HOME HINT: *If you know you are going to have a busy end to your day, with children at after school activities or a late meeting at work, get organized and put the slow cooker on with a tasty treat before you head off in the morning. There is nothing like coming home to the smell of a homemade meal!*

Step 4 Make sure to have your family activity calendar handy when creating your weekly menu so you can make allowances for any evenings that you plan to be out or expect dinner to be late due to children's activities etc. Write the activity that will take place instead of mealtime in that space, for example, 'Dinner with Nanna'.

Step 5 Plan meals that have a good variety of flavors and food groups so that you create a healthy, balanced diet.

HOME HINT: *Budget tip: Have a look at your coupons or grocery store specials for the week. These bargains are a great place to start when deciding what to include in the week's menu!*

Step 6 Include complete meals and snacks for the entire day in your menu plan, including those for every family member. Never assume that you have enough breakfast cereal in the cupboard.

Step 7 Review each recipe in detail and double check that you have the right ingredients in the correct quantities as well. If not, add the items to your grocery list.

HOME HINT: *Budget tip: Whenever possible, make a double batch and freeze the other half (check that the recipe is suitable for freezing first). These are perfect quick meals to have on hand for when you have an unexpected late night.*

Step 8   Make sure each family member has at least one favorite meal on the week's menu.

HOME HINT: *If you have the service available in your area, shop online. Doing so eliminates any impulse purchases and saves you time and money because you are more likely to stick to the list.*

Step 9   Place your weekly menu on your fridge so everyone knows what is on the menu for a given day.

Step 10 Each morning review the menu thoroughly. Take frozen food from the freezer to defrost it and make note of any item you need to pick up fresh that day, such as fish or vegetables.

HOME HINT: *If your weekly menu has been a hit, keep it (and the corresponding shopping list) so you can use it again another week.*

9

HOW TO ORGANIZE MY BATHROOM

Rose has a very unappealing bathroom; it was really the kind of place you wanted to get in and out of very quickly. How can she organize her bathroom so that her three teenage children can use the space, especially when they are all trying to get ready to go out with friends?
At the same time I need to get this space organized so it works for everyone.

Step 1   Set aside 1–2 hours for this project.

Step 2   Grab your supplies:
- Rubber gloves
- Bucket of warm water
- Disinfectant
- Garbage bags

Step 3   Consider the zones/activities you need to account for in your bathroom. Is it a family room with children's bath-time toys or your teenage daughter's makeup studio? What will happen in this bathroom, and what do you need to do to accommodate those activities? Label these as categories.

HOME HINT: *Use plastic storage in the wet areas so they are easy to clean.*

Step 4   Empty out all the cupboards and sort the items into the categories you have selected based on step three.

Step 5   As you sort, throw away anything that is old, moldy or out of date.

HOME HINT: *For help with organizing your medicine cabinet and your makeup, refer to those separate chapters.*

Step 6   Create a separate category for items that don't belong in the bathroom. For example, you may choose to store the towels in your linen closet instead of in your bathroom. Set those items to one side.

Step 7   Once all the cabinets are empty, pull on your rubber gloves, fill your bucket with warm water, add some disinfectant to it, and thoroughly wipe out all the drawers, shelves and containers.

Step 8   Review your storage capacity and allocate areas to your newly created categories.

Step 9   Wipe off all items returning to the cupboards or shelves and store accordingly. Use labels on shelves if necessary to help everyone who uses the bathroom know where items should return to.

HOME HINT: *This is a good time to get creative about how to maximize your storage options. If you have small cupboards, use baskets that you can lift out each time. For example, use one basket for your daily toiletries, such as moisturizer and deodorant, and use a second basket for hair ties and accessories.*

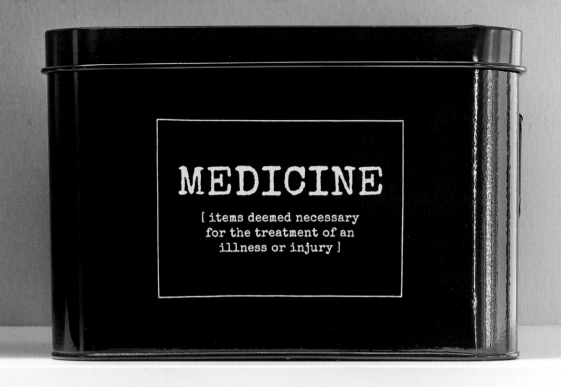

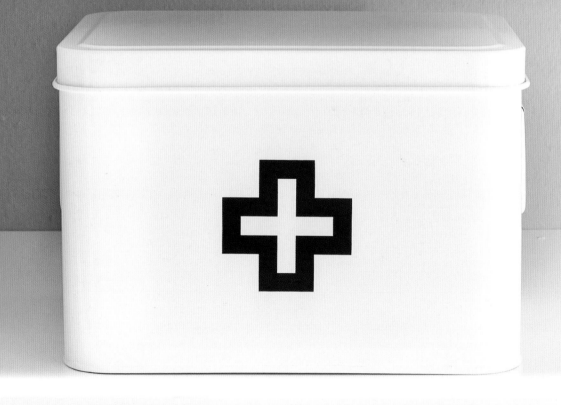

10

HOW TO ORGANIZE MY MEDICINE CABINET

New mum Rebecca was worried about the dangers within the medicine cabinet.
I needed to get this organized so she could keep her family safe!

Where to store your medication?

Medications need to be stored in an area with low humidity and a stable temperature (around room temperature of 68 degrees). The average bathroom does not offer the consistent temperature and low humidity that medications require.

Most drugs will degrade over time, which makes them less effective. Storing them properly is the key to maintaining their effectiveness until the expiration date on the packaging. Keeping them in the bathroom, with its poor temperature and humidity, can be like putting them through an accelerated degradation process.

Step 1 Allow about one hour to do this project. Put a tablecloth on your dining room table. It may be wise to choose a time when the children are not around to avoid any distractions or added risks.

Step 2 Get a garbage bag, a notepad or paper, and small bucket of warm soapy water ready.

Step 3 Gather everything from your existing medicine storage cupboard and take it to your dining room table.

Step 4   Read the labels on all the medications and check the expiration dates. Throw away medication that has expired or those that were needed for a past condition that no longer requires treatment.

HOME HINT: *Use kitty litter to dispose of liquid medications; it will absorb the moisture. Place kitty litter in a sandwich bag, add the liquid medication, seal, then dispose of it.*

Never throw away prescription medication in its bottle. You don't want medication falling into the wrong hands. Keeping the tablets and the bottle separate deters someone from finding a bottle full of the medication in the trash.

Step 5   Wipe off the medication bottles you are keeping with warm, soapy water.

Step 6   Make a list of everyday medical supplies that need replenishing, such as band-aids, aspirin, paracetamol, vitamins, etc.

Step 7   Think about the best place to store your medications. Consider the temperature, humidity, and safety for those with curious little fingers.

HOME HINT: *Avoid those other favorite medicine storage spaces, such as the small cupboard above the oven or the one above the refrigerator. These areas are also affected by temperature fluctuations.*
If you need to store your medication away from children, consider storing it high in the linen cupboard or on a high, but easily accessible, shelf in your pantry.

Step 8   Wipe out the shelves and doors with an antiseptic solution.

Step 9   Categorize your medications, such as Injury (band-aids, antiseptic powder, and bandages), Pain Relief (aspirin, paracetamol, ibuprofen), Prescriptions, and so on.

Step 10 Place each group of medications into separate baskets or containers.

HOME HINT: *Label each basket or container in fun way. My friend, Robin, has hers labelled 'I have an owie', 'I don't feel well', and 'Lotions and potions'.*

HOME HINT: *Never take medication that has expired or that was not prescribed to you.*

Step 11 Return the baskets to your medicine cabinet.

Step 12 If you don't have stackable containers, use a shelf stand to create extra space.

Step 13 Put a reminder in your calendar or diary to do this every six months and your medicine cabinet will always be organized!

11

HOW TO ORGANIZE MY MAKEUP

*Kim is a makeup collector! Every time she opens a magazine or goes shopping,
all those pretty colors seduce her and she buys the latest shade. Kim now has so much makeup
that she can't possibly wear it all. She still has her electric blue mascara from 1985! I need to
help her purge, organize, and update her makeup collection!*

Step 1 Set aside an hour or two for this project (depending upon how much makeup
you own.

Step 2 Clear a large space such as your dining table or kitchen counter.

Step 3 Place all of your makeup in that area, gathering it from all those hiding places in
handbags, cosmetic bags, gym bags; look everywhere.

HOME HINT: *Have you ever had your 'colors' done by a makeup professional? Get that palette out
and keep it on hand. Similarly, you may just know that coral is not your color. Keep that in mind
throughout this process.*

Step 4 Sort the makeup into categories:

- Foundation
- Powders
- Concealers
- Lipstick
- Lip liners

- Eye liners
- Eye shadows
- Mascaras
- Eyebrow pencils
- Blush/rouge

Step 5 Within each group, decide what needs to go. If you don't love it, or it doesn't love you, toss it. Yes, discarding it can be heartbreaking but not as much as a skin infection or the embarrassment of a makeup fashion fail.

Step 6 Give your brushes a good clean with pH neutral soap or your hair shampoo.

Step 7 Throw away any applicators that are deteriorating or beyond cleaning; make a quick note of what you need to replace.

Step 8 Return your final pieces to their original home.

Step 9 Consider if you are storing you items efficiently. There are some great storage options for cosmetics.

How do I know how long to keep it?

You can rate your cosmetics a bit like food. If it smells off, has mold, its color has changed, or it has a film over it, then it's no longer usable. Throw it out, regardless of how much you love it; saving yourself from the skin reaction or infection is much more important.

In the United States, there are now laws that require cosmetic manufacturers to include expiration dates on their product packaging. Guidelines can often be vague, depending upon which magazine or beauty consultant you ask. These recommendations are to be used as a guide, and you should, of course, apply common sense.

Mascara – 3 months
Mascara has the shortest life span of any cosmetic because of the high risk of transferring bacteria between your eye and the tube.

Eye Pencils – up to 2 years
To ensure these are kept in tiptop condition, regularly sharpen them with a clean sharpener.

Eye Shadows: Liquids – around 1 year; Powders – up to 2 years

HOME HINT: *If you have had an eye infection of any type, you must discard any makeup you have used in this area. If you don't, you may continue to transfer the infection between the cosmetic and your eye.*

Lipsticks – up to 2 years

This applies to both lip liners and lipstick tubes. Once again, always be sure to sharpen lip pencils with a clean sharpener to keep them in their best condition.

Blushes and Powders: Creams – no more than 1 year; Powders – no more than 2 years

Check if the blushes are cracked or coming loose from the container. Also, make sure that there are no nasties lurking in your cream products.

Foundations and Concealers – around 18 months

Oil-free foundations may not last quite as long because they have a tendency to dry out.

HOME HINT: *Using clean applicators and sponges will help lengthen the life of your cosmetics. Wash and/or replace these items regularly.*

For further advice and recommendations visit the Food and Drug Administration website, they provide general advice for consumers.

12

HOW TO ORGANIZE MY BEDROOM

Natalie is desperate to create a place where she can rest at the end of the day, but everything seems to get dumped on her bed. She has a hectic schedule and 'doesn't have time' to put things back where they came from. She has been gazing longingly at TV shows where do-it-yourselfers make over bedrooms to look like 5-star hotels. Perhaps, with a bit of organizing, we can help Natalie create her own retreat.

Step 1 It is always best to allow too much time than not enough, so I suggest that you schedule a Saturday morning for this project.

Step 2 Gather supplies:
- Trash bags
- Hampers or containers to sort items into
- Dust cloths
- Bucket of warm water
- Sponge
- Vacuum cleaner

Step 3 Set up hampers into sorting categories. The Traditional Sorting Method outlined in Chapter 4 will work perfectly. You could also include two other hampers; one for 'Dry-Cleaning' and one for 'Mending' (refer to the Chapter on Wardrobe).

Step 4 Start to the left of your door way and work in a clockwise direction around your room. Pick up each item one by one and put it into one of the labelled hampers. Do not be tempted to put things away at this point.

Step 5 Continue around the entire room, when you get to your bed, strip it down to the mattress.

Step 6 You may leave the room to take the sheets and all the bedding to the laundry.

HOME HINT: *Take your duvet/comforter and curtains to the drycleaner, or at least hang them on the line for the day to give them an airing. Also, take the time to turn your mattress.*

Step 7 Once you have completed your 'round' of the room, take your duster and cleaning supplies and give everything a thorough cleaning. Vacuum around all the skirting boards and give the mattress a vacuuming while you are there.

HOME HINT: *Before you put everything away, have you thought about re-arranging the layout of your room, now is the perfect time to give it a try. 'A change is as good as a holiday!'*

Step 8 To deal with the 'Toss' hamper, get those items into a garbage bag and immediately into the trash.

Step 9 Put the 'Donate' hamper, with items to donate or to return to friends, in your car immediately so that you don't have any second thoughts.

Step 10 Take items that do not belong in your bedroom to their correct location – hammers rarely have a use in the bedroom, take them to the garage.

HOME HINT: *To make your drawers more organized, consider expandable drawer dividers. These neatly create two compartments in your drawer to keep your socks and undergarments separate if they are sharing a drawer.*

Step 11 Remake your bed using fresh linen. You may be inspired to get a new comforter cover to give your room a new, serene feel.

Step 12 For the items that are to remain in the room, return them to their correct location.
If you are short on storage, you may need to consider:
1. Whether your bedroom is the best place for the items that you plan to store there? Perhaps they could be stored in another location; or
2. Creating more storage in your room.

Step 13 Continue placing the items into their newly created home until everything is put away.

HOME HINT: *If you have selected solid colored plastic or wicker containers, label them so you know what they contain for easy retrieval. Traditional paper luggage tags look great; they are also very cheap and easy to change.*

You now have a clutter free and clean environment in which to slumber.

13

HOW TO ORGANIZE MY WARDROBE

*Robyn has a lot of clothes, she loves to buy them and she is fantastic at making them!
However, over the past year she has lost a lot of weight and now needs help reorganizing
the space. I need to help Robyn embrace her new size and let go of the old, it is too
overwhelming for her to do alone.*

Step 1   Set aside four hours (minimum) to do this project with no interruptions. Put on some very comfy clothes and have a full length mirror handy.

Step 2   Gather supplies:
- Trash bags
- Hampers or containers to sort items into
- Dust cloths
- Bucket of warm water
- Sponge
- Vacuum cleaner
- Good quality hangers (not wire ones)

HOME HINT: *Using large green garbage bags for trash and white ones for donation will help you to know which bags go where at the end of the project!*

Step 3   Set a goal of how much you want to reduce your wardrobe, for example, 50 percent. Knowing what you are aiming for will keep you focused. Keep reminding yourself of your goal; make it like a mantra throughout the project.

Step 4   Take everything out of your wardrobe, cupboards, drawers and boxes and put them onto your bed.

Step 5   Pick up the first item you see (we are doing this one thing at a time). You are not to let go of this item until you have made a clear decision about it. Here is how to decide; ask yourself the following questions:
- How does it make you feel when you see it?
- How does it make you feel when you put it on?
- Does it fit?
- Does it really suit my body shape?
- Is it worn out or does it need repairing?

- Do I have a similar item that I like better?
- Have I worn it in the last 12 months?
- Does it suit my current lifestyle (i.e. how often do I go to a Gala Ball nowadays)?

HOME HINT: *My dear friends at Penny's Boutique have what they call the 'Smile Test'; if you put something on and it makes you smile, then chances are, you should keep it!*

Step 6 Based on the answers to those questions, move the item into one of the following categories:
- Keep
- Throw away – garbage bag
- Donate – garbage bag
- Mend – into a shopping / carry bag
- Dry cleaning – into a separate shopping / carry bag

HOME HINT: *Mending – make sure the item is worth mending. Is the garment otherwise still in good condition? Would it be cheaper to replace it? Or, have it replicated by a dressmaker?*

Step 7 For items that you want to keep, carefully hang them on a good quality hanger and place them in your wardrobe with the hanger facing inwards, i.e. the hook goes around the back of the pole.

HOME HINT: *In 12 months, see how many hangers are still facing this way. That will let you know what garments you haven't worn in the last year, helping you decide whether to include them in next year's wardrobe.*

Step 8 Hang your items according to garment types, i.e. trousers together, skirts together, long sleeve blouses, short sleeve blouses, and so on.

Step 9 Further sort each of these categories into colors. This will really help you keep track of how many white blouses you own and equally highlight any areas in your wardrobe that are lacking.

Step 10 Repeat this process until you have all the items sorted into the categories and neatly hung in your closet or folded and placed on your shelves/drawers.

Step 11 Take care of the items for donation, garbage, mending and dry cleaning immediately. The sooner removed, the sooner forgotten! As for the mending and dry cleaning, the sooner you get it to the cleaners, the sooner it will be returned so you can enjoy wearing it again!

HOME HINT: *When considering an item for charity, ask yourself, "Would I ask a friend to pay me $5 for it?" If the answer is no then it should be thrown out. Don't use charity as a dumping ground; remember people who need charity also have dignity.*

Step 12 Make a list of items that you need to replace (i.e. the gaps in your wardrobe that may have been identified in Step 9) and keep it in your handbag/wallet for when you are out shopping; you never know when you might spot the item on sale. You can also refer to the list whenever you are tempted to buy clothing; stick to the list items first!

Step 13 Reward yourself with a new item for your wardrobe. Remember, don't buy anything that you already have. If you do, make sure you remove the old item and either donate it, or throw it away!

HOME HINT: *To fold your clothes like a pro, you must get a FlipFOLD®. It's the only way to quickly fold all your clothing to a uniform size in less than five seconds every time. There are two sizes to choose from, one for adult clothing and one for children's.*

14

HOW TO ORGANIZE MY HANDBAGS

Christie is a handbag hoarder. She loves them (don't we all), and every conceivable handbag size, shape, and color have been brought into her collection. Sometimes, they don't get the love they deserve, and some are completely forgotten. I need to help Christie with a complete reorganization of her handbag collection.

Step 1   Allow yourself an hour to complete this task, grab a coffee/wine, and a garbage bag!

Step 2   Gather all your handbags, good, bad and ugly, into one central area – the dining room table is always a good surface for these types of projects.

Step 3   Empty the contents of each handbag onto the table. Surprise! Did you find any missing treasures?

Step 4   Take your empty bags outside or hold them over a sink or garbage can, turn each one upside down, and shake it to clear out any dust, crumbs or other nasties. Get your hand inside and give it a good bash to make sure it is completely clear of debris.

Step 5   Looking at the contents of your bag, grab a garbage bag and quickly get rid of the trash, wrappers and tissues.

HOME HINT: *When buying an everyday bag, think about function, not just fashion. Save your ultra-cool fashion bags for the occasions when you don't have to consider function as much.*

Step 6 Place the remaining items into two simple groups. First, items that don't belong in your bag every day and, second, those that are essential. These essential items are items you absolutely must carry with you every day, i.e. your wallet/pocketbook, some makeup items, business cards, pen, pencil, notepad etc.

HOME HINT: *Only carry a pencil (mechanical pencil) in your handbag. Ink pens too often damage gorgeous leather bags forever. Leather and pens are not friends!*

Step 7 Once you have decided what items are essential, everything that is left should either be put in the trash (if it missed the first round) or returned to its rightful place within your home or office.

HOME HINT: *Clear out your bag of all trash and unnecessary items every day when you get home. Important documents, contact details, or tax receipts are often lost in the bottom of handbags.*

Step 8 Back to the bags; is there anything you can purge here? Inspect each bag to ensure that it is in tip-top condition. Could a professional polish restore a favorite bag? If bags are looking tattered and cannot be repaired, or if they aren't worth the investment of the repair, let them go. If a bag was trendy last season but looks a little dated now, consider donating it or selling it online.

   The aim of this step is to limit your collection to those that are in the best condition, are classics, or are ones that you simply cannot part with.

HOME HINT: *You can often tell how old a handbag is if a smart phone won't fit in the mobile phone pocket!*

Step 9 Once you have selected the bags you wish to keep in your collection, clean them to let their true value shine. It is best to start with a dust cloth or a damp cloth when cleaning vinyl bags. Check care instructions for delicate or leather items.

HOME HINT: *Avoid overloading your handbag; this can have long-term effects on your neck and shoulders.*

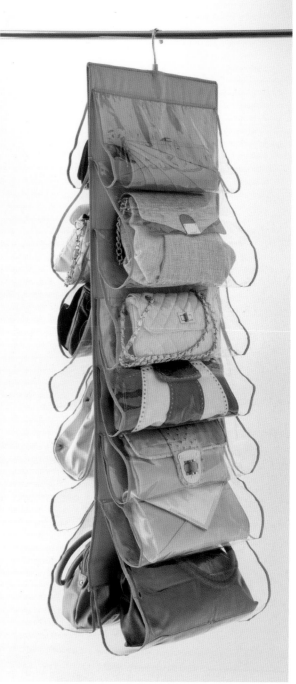

Step 10 If you have many handbags and switch them out often, consider using a handbag organizer, which can help you keep control of your handbag essentials. Such an organizer that you can pop in and out of each bag you use is ideal.

Step 11 Now for storage. The best way to store handbags is in their original dust cover (if they came with one). To help retain their shape, insert a cushion filler into the bag and zip it up.

HOME HINT: *If your bag did not come with a dust cover, invest in some inexpensive pillow slips/pillow cases, which will do the same thing.*

Step 12 Throwing your handbags into the bottom of your wardrobe or closet is a poor way to care for them. If you are short on space, consider using a canvas wardrobe hanger, or line them up neatly under your bed in their dust covers (areas under beds gather dust quickly, so it is essential for them to be in covers).

HOME HINT: *Consider using clear shoe boxes to store evening, delicate or smaller-sized bags. Shoeboxes stack easily or you can slide them under your bed for easy storage.*

Step 13 Practical things to think about when buying your next handbag:
- Do you prefer a hand-held bag or a shoulder bag? For frequent shoppers, shoulder bags are best, as they leave both hands free.
- Do you prefer a single handle or double handle?
- Give serious thought to the usefulness of very large bags, as they can become extremely heavy when full, and even when they aren't full, it's often difficult to find things in them.
- Equally, very small bags may not accommodate everything you have put into your 'handbag essentials' pile.
- Black lining makes it difficult to find things, especially if your wallet, business card holder etc are also black. Lighter-colored linings are best, if you can find them.
- Make sure the bag closes securely.
- Does it have enough internal/external pockets and an internal divider to keep your things well organized? If you have an internal divider, you can place your handbag organizer in one side and use the other side for larger items, i.e. books or magazines.

15

HOW TO ORGANIZE MY SHOES

Perhaps we should call this client Carrie! In fact, her name is Chris, but she has more shoes than Carrie Bradshaw does. So many, in fact, that it would take more than a year to wear each pair once! Needless to say, I need to do a bit of organizing here to make sure she is always putting her best shoe forward.

Step 1 Allow yourself an hour to complete this task. Grab a coffee / wine, and a garbage bag!

Step 2 Gather all your shoes from every corner of your bedroom, living room, car, handbag, gym bag and suitcase.

Step 3 Bring them all to a central place. The dining table is always a good surface for these types of projects.

Step 4 Line all of your shoes up in pairs. Are you missing any? Take another quick look around the house to see if you can find any 'halves' that may still be hiding.

Step 5 Once you have all your pairs, it will become obvious which ones to immediately throw away: shoes that are damaged or missing their partner. Any shoes that have significant scuffs on the toes or a heel that has been 'dragged', (when you slip down a crack in the pavement and catch your heel) really need to go.

HOME HINT: *Nothing says 'unprofessional' more than a scruffy pair of shoes or dirty nails.*

Step 6 Now, give the rest a serious inspection and ask yourself:
- What is their condition?
- Do they require repair? If so, is it worth it?
- How do they make you feel when you wear them?
- Are they comfortable or are they killers?
- Have they moved out of fashion?

This is the tough moment when you have to categories your shoes:
- Keep
- Repair
- Donate
- Throw

HOME HINT: *Only donate or sell shoes that are in excellent condition, preferably in their original box. Not many people like to walk in other people's sweaty shoes!*

Step 7 Do any shoes need new heels or tips? Consider whether it is worth the investment to have them repaired. If so, grab a bag and place them inside, ready to take to the shoe repair store.

Step 8 For those that do not require repairs, determine which need cleaning and clean them all as appropriate, using special leather or suede cleaner and other cleaners for different types. If you are unsure, your shoe repair store will be able to help you.

Step 9 Closely examine all the shoes you have retained to ensure that they are in their very best condition and ready for storage. Check to see that all beads and embellishments are intact, and that all buckles and hardware are in good working order.

HOME HINT: *Remember to review your athletic shoes too; the supportive soles and lining of trainers will wear out over a 12-month period (depending upon how active you are). Continuing to use trainers that are worn can lead to foot injury.*

Step 10 Now, to store them all. There is a multitude of ways to store your shoes, from the very basic to the outright glamorous. Your storage options largely depend on how much space you have available. Options include:

- The original box with a photo of the shoes stuck to the outside
- Clear shoe boxes; inexpensive and easy to stack
- Open shoe racks; easy to grab on the go, but leaves them open to dust
- Recycle a china cabinet or glass front book shelf to display them

Step 11 Throwing shoes into the bottom of your wardrobe is a poor way to care for them. If you are short on space, consider a canvas wardrobe hanger, or place them in dust covers and line them up neatly under your bed (the area under the bed gathers dust quickly so it is essential to keep them in covers).

HOME HINT: *For evening wear or delicate shoes, consider using clear shoe boxes for storage. They will also stack easily or slide under your bed for easy storage.*

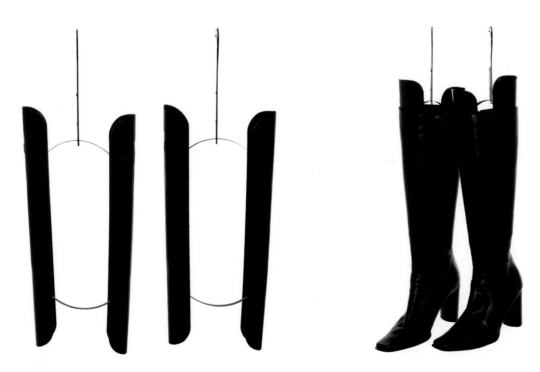

16

HOW TO ORGANIZE MY JEWELRY AND ACCESSORIES

Kathryn loves to dress up and that includes wearing and owning many pieces of costume jewelry, accessories and especially hats! Her beads are a tangled mess of 'spaghetti beads' and need immediate rescuing! I need to get them organized so Kathryn can share them with the world.

Step 1   Allow yourself at least an hour to complete this task; grab a coffee / wine.

Step 2   Gather some supplies:
- Jewelry tools if you have any, such as small pliers or tweezers
- Small dishes to keep track of loose beads
- Compartment containers and / or any jewelry organizers you have
- Super glue or craft glue for making repairs
- Notepad and paper

Step 3   Gather all your accessories from every corner of your bedroom, bathroom, car, handbag, gym bag and suitcase.

Step 4   Bring all of the items to a central place – the dining table is always a good surface for these types of projects.

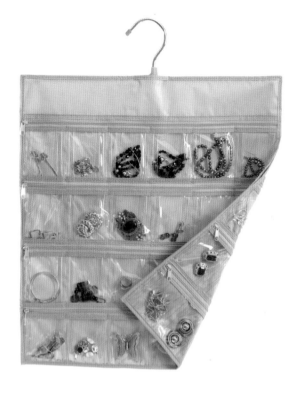

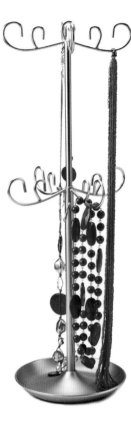

Step 5 Take some time to untangle all of the accessories and sort them
- Necklaces
- Earrings
- Bracelets/bangles
- Rings
- Hats/feathers
- Watches
- Scarves
- Belts
- Hats

Step 6 Sort the necklaces, checking to make sure that all the beads are present and that no links are broken.

Step 7 Make sure you have pairs of earrings and the corresponding backs for pierced earrings.

HOME HINT: *If you have a few pieces of expensive jewelry, now might be a good time to have them professionally appraised for insurance purposes.*

Step 8 Check that all bracelets and bangles are in good repair, with no broken links or missing embellishments.

Step 9 Check to see that all rings have their stones and embellishments in place.

Step 10 If you find missing pieces or broken items, decide if they should be replaced or repaired? Are they worth the time and effort to fix them? If so grab your tools and start your basic repairs.

HOME HINT: *It is best to leave the repairs of precious pieces of jewelry to a professional. This includes having replacement gems fitted.*

Step 11 Check that watches are in full working order, some may require a battery change, others may require a full repair.

Step 12 Check belts to ensure that they are not cracked (this usually happens beside the most regularly used buckle hole) or that the holes and buckle are in good repair. Anything that does not look its best should be tossed.

Step 13 Check hats and scarves for general condition. Some perhaps need washing. Perhaps some need mending. Sort accordingly.

Step 14 Now that you can see the items you have (including those in need of repair), consider which items you want to keep and which ones you want to sell or donate. Naturally, throw away broken items that cannot be reasonably repaired if they are low value costume pieces. Otherwise, consider selling any that have value.

Step 15 Make a note of any beads, embellishments or fasteners you need to replace.

HOME HINT: *Given the popularity of beading, you may be able to find suitable replacements for lost pieces at bead shops. Take your broken piece with you; they may even fix it for you on the spot.*

Step 16 Take your cleaners out and give any precious metals a polish. You can clean many plastic items by using soapy water, rinsing, and leaving them to dry outdoors for a few hours.

HOME HINT: *You can effectively clean some precious metals by dropping them into a glass of water with denture cleaning tablets.*

Step 17 Now for jewelry storage. There are many ways to store your accessories. Even a quick look at Google or Pinterest can provide plenty of inspiration for storage options, from DIY projects to high end and even custom solutions. The best solution will greatly depend on the types of accessories you have most of in your collection.

Step 18 Hats, particularly those that are delicate, should be stored in an air tight container with the crown stuffed with tissue paper. Make sure the hat is absolutely dry first; you don't want any mold growing.

Step 19 Scarves can be stored on a tie rack or folded neatly into a drawer or decorative storage box.

Step 20 Roll belts and place them in a drawer or loop them over a coat hanger or a specialist belt hanger.

17

HOW TO ORGANIZE MY CHILDREN'S BEDROOMS

Helen is a very busy mom with an equally busy 7 year old son. He loves to play in his bedroom and the living room. His bedroom is a combination of sleep, homework and play area. I need to help Helen create some organization in the space before he returns to school for the new term.

Step 1 It is always best to allow too much time rather than not enough, so I suggest doing this project on a school day when the children are away.

Step 2 Gather supplies:
- Garbage bags
- Hampers or containers to sort items into
- Dust cloths
- Bucket of warm water
- Sponge
- Vacuum cleaner

Step 3 Set up hampers into sorting categories, (refer to Chapter 4, The Basics of Decluttering). The easiest sorting method for this project is the Traditional Method. You could also include an extra hamper for 'Mending' (refer to Chapter 13, How to Organize My Wardrobe).

Step 4 Set up sorting bins for toys, such as action figures, electronics, board games, blocks/building, dolls, dress up and crafts, for example.

HOME HINT: *If you are donating clothing to specific children, you may want to create additional storage tubs or hampers labeled by size and gender. For example, Boys Size 5, Girls Size 10, etc. This will help the charity easily sort your items, or if you plan on passing along to friends or family, they are readily organized.*

Step 5 Start to the left of the door way and work in a clockwise direction around your room. Pick up each item one by one and put into labelled hampers. Do not be tempted to put things away at this point.

Step 6 Continue around the entire room; when you get to the bed, strip it down to the mattress.

Step 7 You may leave the room to take the sheets and all the bedding to the laundry.

HOME HINT: *Take the duvet/comforter and curtains to the drycleaner, or at least hang them on the line for the day to give them an airing. Also, take the time to turn the mattress.*

Step 8 Once you have completed your 'round' of the room, take your duster and cleaning supplies and give everything a thorough cleaning. Vacuum around all the skirting boards and give the mattress a vacuuming while you are there.

HOME HINT: *Before you put everything away, have you thought about re-arranging the layout of the room, now is the perfect time to give it a try. It might be the perfect time to add a desk for homework.*

Step 9 Deal with the 'Toss' hamper, by getting those items into a garbage bag immediately and into the trash.

Step 10 Put the donate hamper, with items to donate to charity or to return to friends, in your car immediately so that you don't have any second thoughts.

Step 11 Inspect the items that were sorted into the 'Toy' bins; check for items that might be broken or have missing parts. Decide if the toy is still safe, useable or repairable. If not throw it away.

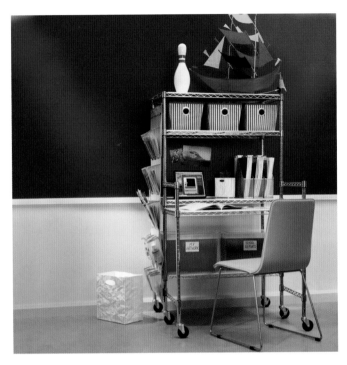

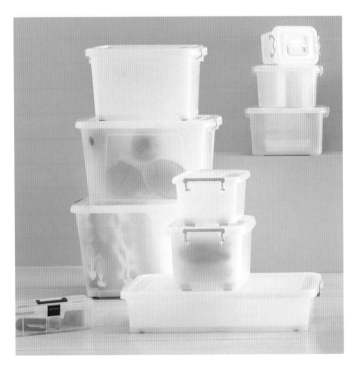

HOME HINT: *If there are toys that your child has outgrown, decide what you are going to do with them. If they are in good condition, consider passing them on to a younger brother or sister, a cousin, or a family friend, or donate them to a local charity or woman's shelter.*

Step 12 Next, take items that do not belong in the bedroom to their correct location – skateboards rarely have a use in the bedroom, take it to the garage.

HOME HINT: *If you have a secondary toy or play area in the home, keep all similar games together. For example, keep all gaming consoles and gear by the TV.*

Step 13 Remake the bed using fresh linen.

Step 14 Return the items that are to remain in the room to their correct storage location.

Step 15 Make sure organization tools are easy to use and at the child's level. For example, install low hooks to accommodate book bags, hats, bags, scarves, and more on the back of the door or elsewhere in the rooms. Another important idea, especially for children who are too young to read, is to label storage solutions with both pictures and words. Keep storage for children at child-friendly height and visibility.

Step 16 Continue placing items into their newly created home until everything is put away.

18

HOW TO ORGANIZE MY KIDS' TOYS

Busy Mom, Kelly, is completely overwhelmed with her son's building bricks. There are so many pieces; who knows what set they belong to anymore. Can I help her organize these and all the other toys that are overflowing from the toy room cupboards? Her house resembles a childcare center more than a family home.

The number of children, their ages, and their interest will factor into determining how long this project will take but allow at least few hours to be on the safe side.

If your children are old enough, let them know what you are planning ahead of time.

HOME HINT: *Choose one time of year to cull. I always say October because it leads nicely into "we need to make space for the new things Santa will bring you." Helen Butler, Clutter Rescue.*

Step 1 Ahead of time, ask your Children to select a few toys that they have outgrown and that other children may like to own. Set those aside, ready for donation.

HOME HINT: *You may find it easier to complete the remainder of the project when your children are at school or when they are on a play date.*

Step 2 Gather supplies:
- Tubs/boxes/containers
- Pen
- Notepad
- Garbage bags

Step 3 Think about where you want to store the toys at the completion of the project. Are they going into the bedrooms, the living room or a combination of both?

Select a suitable 'zone' for each toy type; for example, bats and balls may be stored in the garage, soft toys in the bedroom, electronic games in the living room.

Write down the zones you have selected for each toy type.

HOME HINT: *Boys and girls toys have slightly different organizing needs because girls' toys usually have many little bits (e.g. handbags, shoes, babies, dress ups). Boys' toys are usually larger.*

Step 4 Gather all toys into one room; you may choose the garage floor or the living room for this project. Choose somewhere with a large amount of space, where you have plenty of room to spread out and sort.

Step 5   Make labels for each carton or cardboard box, i.e. bricks, dolls, electronic toys, games.

Step 6   Set aside garbage bags for 'donations' and 'trash'.

Step 7   Start sorting the toys into the designated groups. While sorting, consider the following for each toy:
  • Is it broken or damaged? Throw it away.
  • Is it age appropriate? If not, consider donating it.
  • Does your child still enjoy it? If not, consider donating it.

Step 8   Once you have sorted the toys that you want to retain into their various boxes or containers, review the zones for each category as noted in Step 2. Will all of the toys fit in the designated area? Do you have the correct storage? You may require different sized storage solutions for different toy types, i.e. small storage for doll's clothes, large containers for building blocks.

Step 9   Label each container with words and pictures to help your child identify where to return the toys once they have finished playing.

HOME HINT: *Display prized toys or those that have been constructed or created, i.e. artwork, completed building block projects.*

Step 10 Immediately throw away the toys deemed as trash so that little fingers can't retrieve them.

Step 11 Perhaps include your children in the experience of donating the toys they no longer want or need to other children in need.

HOME HINT: *Make donating outgrown or unused toys an annual event – make it fun. Learn about the gift of giving.*

19

HOW TO ORGANIZE MY LIVING/DINING ROOM

Paige has a busy life and her living and dining rooms are like thoroughfares. Everything that comes into the home is dumped in this area. There is no room on the dining table to share family meals and no room on the sofas for the five members of her family – so much for having a 'family room'. My job is to get rid of the clutter and to create a space for her family to be together in.

This project will happen in four stages.

Stage 1 – Preparing to Organize

Step 1   Schedule 1–2 hours for Stage 1.

Step 2   Sit down in your living room and think about what activities happen in this area. For example, watching TV, eating meals, reading, playing with toys and so on.

HOME HINT: *When thinking about the best place for a zone, consider where the family uses certain items so that the zones are the most efficient use of space. For example, create a space near the TV for DVDs and games. Create a zone near the sofa for books and magazines. Create a zone near the dining table for linens and tableware.*

Step 3   Evaluate your space to determine if you realistically have enough designated zones (areas) to undertake each of these activities. If you don't, you may need to consider moving some of those activities to another area within your home (space permitting). Prioritize the activities within the area in order of importance.

HOME HINT: *Do not rush out and buy any supplies at this stage. This includes furniture and storage solutions. Once you de-clutter and organize your new zones, you may find that you don't need as many new supplies as you thought or that you may have bought the wrong ones.*

Once you have your list of zones written down and know where items will ideally be stored at the completion of this project, you have finished Stage 1.

Stage 2 – Start Sorting

Now that you have considered what activities will take place in this area, you can commence sorting through the items.

Step 1 Gather supplies:
- Garbage bags
- Boxes/bins/hampers
- Pen and paper

Step 2   Label the boxes/hampers according to the zones and/or categories. For example:
- DVDs
- CDs
- Magazines
- Toys/board games
- Electrical cables
- Linens
- Serving ware

Step 3 Label additional boxes/hampers 'donate' and 'another room' (to be moved to another room in the house).

Step 4 Sort every item in the room into one of the labeled boxes or, if trash, into a garbage bag.

HOME HINT: *If you need some help sorting, refer to Chapter 4, The Basics of Decluttering.*

Step 5 Once you have sorted all the items, leave them in the boxes or hampers until after you review Stage 3.

Stage 3 – Furniture Layout and Function

Now that you have your zones, and have cleared the space, you may want to try new furniture layouts in the space. Moving furniture all day simply may not be possible to manage on your own, so try this solution first.

Step 1 Schedule 1–2 hours for this Stage.

Step 2 Gather supplies:
- Pencil
- Eraser
- Paper
- Scale ruler
- Scissors
- Scotch tape

Step 3 Measure the dimensions of your room, remembering to note the windows and doorways. Transfer these measurements to paper, making a floor plan to scale. For example if your room is 5m by 7m, your scale of 1:100 is a shape measuring 50cm by 70cm.

HOME HINT: *Not sure how to do this? Use the search term "How to draw a floor plan to scale." There are several step-by-step guides on the internet as well as video tutorials that demonstrate this step.*

Step 4 Measure the pieces of furniture in your room and make scale cut outs of them, for example if your dining table is 1,800mm x 900mm, cut out a rectangle that measures 18mm x 9mm (this means your furniture is now scaled down to 1:100). Do this with everything in your room (using the same scale, of course).

Step 5 Take the cut-outs of your furniture and move them around your scale room floor plan to see if you can configure it to work better for you.

HOME HINT: *Be sure to make allowances for windowsills, and to ensure that any doors can fully open. Furniture doesn't have to be up against a wall; lounges can be used to divide a room and rugs can be used to define areas too – play around with all the different options*

Step 6 Once you have chosen a furniture layout, tape the furniture pieces to the scale room plan, so you don't forget. You can also use it to show your helpers where to place the furniture.

Stage 4 – Bring It All Together

Now that you have your items sorted into categories and your furniture layout organized, you can make a start on the final stage.

Step 1 Take this opportunity to give your room a thorough cleaning, especially if you are moving furniture. Vacuum and dust all those areas you haven't been able to reach for some time.

Step 2 Move the furniture according to the plan you created in Stage 3.

HOME HINT: *If you are unable to move the furniture on your own, most moving companies will do what is called an 'internal move' for you at an hourly rate.*

Step 3 Place your categorized items in their zones, as outlined in Stage 1.

Step 4 Take the box of items labelled 'donate' immediately to your car for delivery.

Step 5 Take the trash out to the garbage immediately so that nothing creeps back into the home (other family members may not consider it trash).

HOME HINT: *It is really easy to stop the project now and do the rest later. However, spending those extra few moments to completely finishing the job will reap the greatest reward.*

Step 6 Return the items in the 'another room' bin, to their rightful place.

20

HOW TO ORGANIZE MY HOME OFFICE

Sophie had moved three times in four years and had never gotten around to setting up her home office in that time. This meant that all her documents from the past several years were still in boxes and that any new mail or documents had been thrown into piles wherever they landed.

It wasn't until Sophie finally had to face the need to prepare the last five years income tax returns that she realized what a mess she was in. Where were all the receipts? What about the log book for her car? I had to take action and fast!

This project will happen in 6 stages. It might be beneficial to read the entire chapter before you commence so you can plan ahead.

Stage 1 – Evaluate the Space

Step 1 Schedule 1–2 hours for this stage.

Step 2 Grab your supplies:
- Notepad and pen
- Garbage bags

Step 3 Sit down in your office and think about what activities happen in this area. For example, paying bills, kid's homework/study, perhaps you are doing studies of your own, downloading music, storage for your tech devices, and so on.

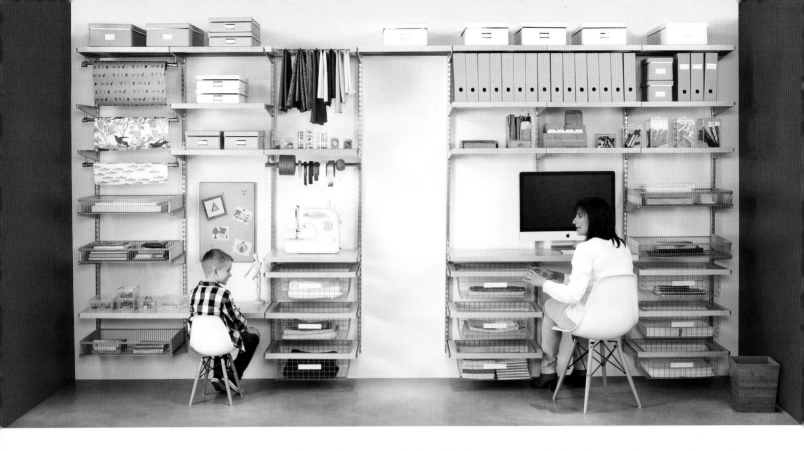

Step 4 Evaluate your space and see if you realistically have enough designated zones (areas) to undertake these activities. If you don't, you may need to consider moving some of those activities to another area within your home (space permitting). Prioritize the activities in order of importance within the office area.

Step 5 Once you have designated zones for your activities, write them down on your notepad. For example, Desk Area (bill payment, homework), Filing Cabinet (household filing), Cupboard (stationery storage).

HOME HINT: *Do not rush out and buy any supplies at all at this stage. This includes furniture, stationery and office supplies. Once you de-clutter and organize your new zones, you may find that you don't need as many new supplies as you thought or that you may have bought the wrong supplies.*

Once you have written down your list of zones and determined where items will ideally be stored at the completion of this project, you have finished Stage 1.

HOME HINT: *If you have plenty of shelving, consider making that your filing zone. You can put your filing into three-ring binders. If you don't have any space for shelving, consider whether there is space under your desk for a two drawer filing cabinet. Note: We will discuss how to file your documents in the next stage. For now, just make sure you have correctly allocated your zones.*

Stage 2 – Sort the paperwork

Step 1   Depending upon how much paper you have allowed to pile up, you should allow from 3–8 hours to do this stage. That seems like a long time, I know, but it will be worth it.

Step 2   Grab your supplies:
- Notepad and pen
- Garbage bags
- 4 large tubs or boxes

Step 3   Create a work space that is comfortable (but not too comfortable). For example, the dining room table, living room floor or a spare bedroom.

Step 4   Gather all the paper that is lurking around your home. Collect it from the top of the fridge, on the kitchen counter, beside your bed, everywhere. Even check your car! Filing is about retrieval, not about putting it away. You are keeping documents in case you need them again, so you must file them in a way that makes it easy to retrieve them when needed.

Step 5   Put all the paper you have found into a box/tub. Don't worry if there is something important in it that you simply must do tomorrow; you will get to it soon.

Step 6   Set up the work area, beginning with three boxes labeled as follows:

Box 1 is for Action
In this box you should place any item of paper that requires your action, for example, a bill to be paid, a contact to be updated, a birthday card to be sent, and so on. Do not put items to be filed in this box; those go in the next one.

Box 2 is for Filing

This box is for all items that you need to retain for future reference so they should be filed; for example, paid bills, birth certificates, medical records, documents for taxation, investment reports, retirement fund documents, and so on.

Box 3 is for Projects

In this box, place all documentation relating to a project that has a start and end date. For example you may have been collecting images for a kitchen renovation, or real estate research for an investment property, or images of products and services for a wedding and so on.

Finally set up a trash bin and make it big!

HOME HINT: *If you are concerned about throwing personal information into the trash (worried about identity theft), consider taking it to or hiring a professional document destruction service.*

Step 7   Now, let's begin. Take each piece of paper, one by one and place it into Box 1, Box 2, or Box 3... or it goes in the trash.

Step 8   Keep going. This is the tough part, so you need to do it as quickly as possible. Perhaps set the kitchen timer for 15-minute intervals. Each time the buzzer goes off, take a 2-minute break, reset the timer, and go for it again. Just keep at it and it will be done before you know it.

You will now have all your paper sorted into the three categories and, hopefully, a full trash bin.

Stage 3 – Action and File the Paperwork

In this section, I am going to show you how to use a basic filing system based on categories. Of course, there are many different methods of filing, but this one is foolproof. If you would like to explore different methods that may suit you better, just look online.

Step 1 Let's start with the items in 'Box 1: Action'. These are the papers that ordinarily belong in your 'inbox' on your desk.

Set aside the next 45 minutes to take action systematically on each item one after another; pay the bill, make the dental appointment, and so forth. In the future, the only papers that should be placed in the inbox are those items that require action.

Step 2 With Box 1 complete, it is time to move on to 'Box 2: Filing'. On your desk, these papers ordinarily belong in a tray marked 'filing'.

Set aside the next 45 minutes to file these items away. During Stage 1, you will have established the type of filing system that will suit your space, either suspension filing or filing in binders.

Step 3 Label the manila folders or dividers with generic titles that suit your household, such as those listed below:
- Finance
- Investments
- Insurances
- Vehicles / Boats / Trailers
- Household Utilities
- School / College
- Medical
- Identification (birth certificates, marriage certificates, passports etc.)

Create as many as you need but don't break it down too much. For example with Household Utilities, at this stage you don't need to go as far as creating a separate file for Gas, Electricity, Water and Cable. Just keep the categories broad and generic to get you started.

Step 4 When the filing is done, it is time to move on to 'Box 3: Project's. These are documents and clippings you are keeping for a specific event or activity.

Set aside 45 minutes to file these items away. Again, during Stage 1, you will have established the type of filing system that will suit your space, either suspension filing

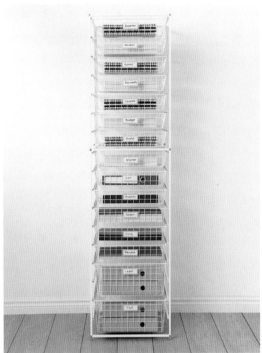

or filing in binders.

Step 5 Label the manila folders or dividers with generic titles that suit your household, such as those listed below:
- Bathroom renovation
- Overseas holiday
- College research

For smaller or bulk items, you may want to include some plastic sleeves or pockets to keep these items neat.

HOME HINT: *If you have adequate storage, you may choose to create boxes for your projects instead of files.*

Stage 4 – Decluttering

Now, let's move along to other parts of your Home Office. Let's work through the non-paper items.

Step 1   You should set aside around two hours for this stage.

Step 2   Grab your supplies:
  • Notepad and pen
  • Garbage bags
  • 4 large tubs or boxes

Step 3   Create a flat work space. For example the dining room table.

Step 4   The items you have remaining will probably fall into one of the following groups:
  • Stationery
  • Office supplies
  • Electrical devices
  • Electrical cables

  • CDs
  • Books
  • Existing files

Step 5 Separate all the items into groups, like-with-like. For example, one tub of stationery, one tub of electrical devices, and so on.

HOME HINT: *If you have a pile of cables that you just don't know what they belong to, take the time to try and marry them up with their correct devices. Once you have made the right match, label the cable accordingly.*

Step 6 As you handle each item, decide if you still need it and if it is still relevant. For example, you probably don't need a power charger for a mobile phone you no longer own, so it can be thrown away. If you have an old printer that no longer works, is it worth having it repaired? If not, then perhaps it's time to throw it away or donate it.

   If you have items that are in good working order but you don't need them, or if you have items that you are unsure about, put them into a separate container (we will come back to these).

HOME HINT: *Check your local newspaper or City Hall to see if they have a recommended way for recycling or throwing away computer items.*

Step 7 Once you have completed sorting these items, everything in your office space should be in containers, with the exception of your desk, chair and computer – right? Take some time to clean things up and wipe down your desk, drawers and shelves and get ready for the next stage.

Step 5 – Bring it Together

Step 1 Go back to the list of your zones that you created in Stage 1 to help you decide where to store each item.

Step 2 Put the filing items away, either in their filing cabinet or on a shelf.

Step 3 Place the 'kept' items from the declutter stage in their proper zones.

Step 4 Make a note of any extra storage supplies you may need to complete the project and set a firm time in your calendar to shop for these additional items and finish the organizing.

You should now have a super-organized home office that is functional and easy to work in.

HOME HINT: *Recommended reading: If you are keen to set up a super slick filing system in your Home Office, I highly recommend that you get a copy of* Paperflow *by Maryanne Bennie and Brigitte Hinneberg.*

21

HOW TO ORGANIZE MY INBOX

Tracie had over 4,000 messages in her email inbox and never had any time to sort through them, so she just kept letting them add up, keeping all messages – just in case! She needed strategies to help her get it organized.

I am going to challenge you to change the way you think about your email's inbox; to think about it as a portal for receiving information much like voicemail or a fax machine. You wouldn't leave 4,000 messages sitting on your voicemail would you? You would receive the message, action it, and delete it, right? I think that you should think about using your email's inbox in a similar way.

Step 1 Set aside at least an hour to complete this task, depending upon how many messages you need to organize.

Step 2 Create three top level folders
- ACTION – items that require action, such as bills, or replies.
- FILING – items that you need to retain for future reference.
- PROJECTS – items that pertain to specific projects.

HOME HINT: *If you have just organized your home office, these categories will look familiar – for a good reason. Replicate the same filing system across all platforms so you only have to learn one method.*

Step 3   Under ACTION, create a few sub-folders that describe the action that needs to happen, such as 'Bills to Pay', 'Articles to Read' and so forth.

Step 4   The FILING is for items that need to be retained for future reference. If this is purely for your home environment, you may create sub-folders titled 'School', 'Vouchers', 'Holiday', and so forth.

HOME HINT: *I don't recommend that you file client correspondence in this way. Save all documents that are relevant to your company's document management system in a way that everyone working on that client has access to the information. This will ensure that your own inbox isn't choked with unnecessary emails.*

For example, if you use Outlook:
1.   *Open the email message*
2.   *Select File*
3.   *Select Save As*
4.   *Navigate to the client folder it needs to be saved in*
5.   *Ensure you have selected the 'Save' type as 'Outlook Email Format'*
6.   *You may then delete the email from your inbox, it is now stored in your clients folder.*

If you are not using Outlook, check your own email system for the relevant file saving options.

Step 5   Items that pertain to specific projects that have a start and end date belong in the PROJECTS folder; for example, a house renovation project or the development of a website. Set up sub folders within this folder for each separate project.

Retaining this key information in your personal inbox could potentially be disastrous – think about the 'hit by a bus' scenario – how would other members of your team access key information in your inbox if it is not correctly filed and / or stored?

Step 6   If you already have folders created that fit into these categories, move them into these folders now. Just drag and drop.

Step 7   It's time to start going through your inbox. It is better to start at the oldest messages and work your way through to the current date. Delete or move messages to the appropriate category and/or subfolder as you go.

HOME HINT: *You can speed this process up by sorting messages by Sender. If all the emails coming from Mary Smith pertain to one specific project, you can select all of these messages and save them at the same time to the correct file. You can use the same method when sorting by Subject.*

Step 8   Schedule a regular time to empty your 'deleted items' box – this doesn't automatically happen.

HOME HINT: *Delete all the emails that pertain to an event (such as "Dad's 60th birthday") once the event is over. Removing emails that are no longer relevant keeps the inbox clear.*

Step 9   Schedule a regular time to check your 'junk email' box – non-junk mail sometimes ends up here.

HOME HINT: *Create rules within your email system to have newsletters or circulars directed to the 'Items to Read' folder, in the 'Recurring Action' folder, for future reading.*

The key is to keep your inbox to a manageable size so you can see all the contents of your Inbox on your screen (you don't have to scroll down to see any items). It can be done. Start a habit of quickly checking your inbox every afternoon before you shut down your computer to ensure that everything has been actioned or filed.

As with any system like this, there will always be something that doesn't quite fit into any category or specific action. There might be an urgent email you need to leave in your inbox so you don't forget to do something.

Some people are more visual than others are and might not feel comfortable moving it out of the inbox. This is still OK. However, I recommend you assign it a category color, red is best for urgent, so it stands out. Remember to use that color only for things that are truly urgent. Once you have completed the action, immediately move it out of the inbox.

HOME HINT: *Every few months export your contacts to a 'cloud' storage system, or an Excel spreadsheet and save it to your hard drive.*

22

HOW TO ORGANIZE MY LAUNDRY ROOM

Kay is a busy Mom who is in her laundry room every day. She has just moved into a new home and the storage options and layout is very different to her old house. This space needs to function for her for washing, folding, ironing, cleaning shoes and storing household cleaning products. She needs my help to create a new laundry space that suits her needs.

This project will happen in three stages.

Stage 1 – Evaluate the Space

Step 1   Set aside 1–2 hours for this stage.

Step 2   Think about the activities that happen in this area and write them down. For example, washing, ironing, mud room, storage and so on.

Step 3   Evaluate your space to see if you realistically have enough designated zones (areas) to undertake these activities. If you don't, you may need to consider moving some of those activities to another area within your home (such as the garage). Prioritize the activities within the area in order of importance.

HOME HINT: *Do not rush out and buy any supplies at this stage. This includes furniture and storage solutions. Once you de-clutter and organize your new zones, you may find that you don't need as many new supplies as you thought or that you may have bought the wrong ones.*

Once you have your list of Zones written down and have decided where the items will ideally be stored at the completion of this project, you have finished Stage 1.

Stage 2 – Sorting

Now that you have considered the activities that will take place in this area, you can commence sorting through the items.

Step 1   Gather supplies:
- Garbage bags
- Boxes/hampers
- Pen and paper

Step 2 Label boxes / hampers according to the zones and / or categories.
For example:
- Cleaning supplies
- Dusters
- Shoe cleaners
- Sewing repairs
- Household tools

Step 3 Label additional boxes / hampers for 'donate' and 'another room' (to be moved to another room in the house).

Step 4 Sort every item in the laundry room into one of the labeled boxes or, if trash, into a garbage bag. Once all items are sorted, let them remain in the boxes or hampers until the next stage.

HOME HINT: *If you need some help sorting, refer to Chapter 4, The Basics of De-cluttering.*

Stage 3 – Bring it together

Step 1 Take this opportunity to clean the laundry room thoroughly. It is often a very dusty place, especially if you have a tumble dryer.

HOME HINT: *Plastic containers and wire rack systems are perfect for laundry rooms. They are easy to clean and are less likely to get moldy. Wall mounted rack systems make the best use of vertical spaces.*

Step 2   Review the items that need to be stored in the space and the designated Zones you created in Stage 1. Ensure that they will work as you envisioned.

Step 3   Label all storage containers for easy retrieval.

Step 4   Store items in their designated zones.

Step 5   Make a list of any additional storage items you need to complete the project.

Step 6   Make a firm time in your diary to obtain these extra items and complete the project.

23

HOW TO ORGANIZE MY LINEN CUPBOARD

Shirley has an amazing linen cupboard; she has more space than she knows what to do with, which is part of the problem. Every time a member of the household doesn't know where to put something, the response is always, 'put it in the linen cupboard'. After years of this, Shirley's once pristine linen cupboard now resembles a junk cupboard.

Step 1 Set aside around four hours to do this project with no interruptions. Ensure you have a good sorting space nearby to work in; the master bed is often a good work surface to use for this project.

Step 2 Gather supplies:
- Garbage bags
- Hampers or containers to sort items into
- Dust cloths
- Bucket of warm water
- Sponge
- Vacuum cleaner

HOME HINT: *Using large green garbage bags for trash and white garbage bags for donation will help you know which bags go where at the end of the project.*

Before

After

Step 3 Take everything from your linen cupboard to your sorting area.

Step 4 Sort items in to categories, for example:

- Sheets
- Blankets
- Comforters
- Towels

- Beach towels
- Tea towels
- Hand towels
- Table linen

HOME HINT: *Do you have more towels than a 5-Star Hotel? If you do, and they are in good condition, donate them. Shelters for the homeless are always grateful to receive more linens.*

Step 5   Review all the items and assess their quality. Throw away those that have damage or are threadbare.

Step 6   Put all sheet sets together, making sure you have the matching pillowcases too.

HOME HINT: *Before you throw away any worn out linen, consider cutting them down for dusters. If you have no need for more dusters, take them to your local mechanic; they love rags.*

Step 7   Carefully fold all the items you want to retain into a uniform size. A FlipFOLD® is especially good at folding towels (as well as your clothes).

Step 8   Take this opportunity to clean your linen cupboard completely. Wipe/dust all the shelves and vacuum the floor area.

Step 9   Return items to the linen cupboard in groups; one shelf for sheets, one for towels, etc.

HOME HINT: *Storage ideas:*
- *Allocate each member of the household a color, that way you know which linen belongs to which bed.*
- *Fold fitted and flat sheets and one pillowcase of a set and place all these items into the remaining pillowcase for easy storage.*
- *Use storage boxes and label them with bed sizes, such as Queen, Double, Single.*

Step 10 Consider using clearly labeled stackable storage containers for easy retrieval of non-linen items that are to be stored in the linen cupboard.

Step 11 Return all the remaining items to their correct location within your home.

Step 12 Place throwaway items in the trash and the 'donate' and 'give away' items in your car for quick delivery!

24

HOW TO ORGANIZE MY SEWING ROOM

Dorothy is a keen seamstress; she makes everything from curtains to dresses for her granddaughters. Adding to that, her husband John is an upholsterer who has his own collection of fabrics and threads. They need my help to get everything organized so that projects are easy to start and finish.

Step 1   Gather all sewing supplies and associated items into the sewing room.

Step 2   Gather sorting supplies:
- Baskets/hampers/boxes (for sorting)
- Scissors to trim any ends or edges

Step 3   Create categories to suit your sewing hobbies and needs; for example:
- Quilting
- Needlework
- Clothing
- Patterns
- Threads
- Embellishments
- Ribbons

Step 4   Sort your materials into the categories you have created.

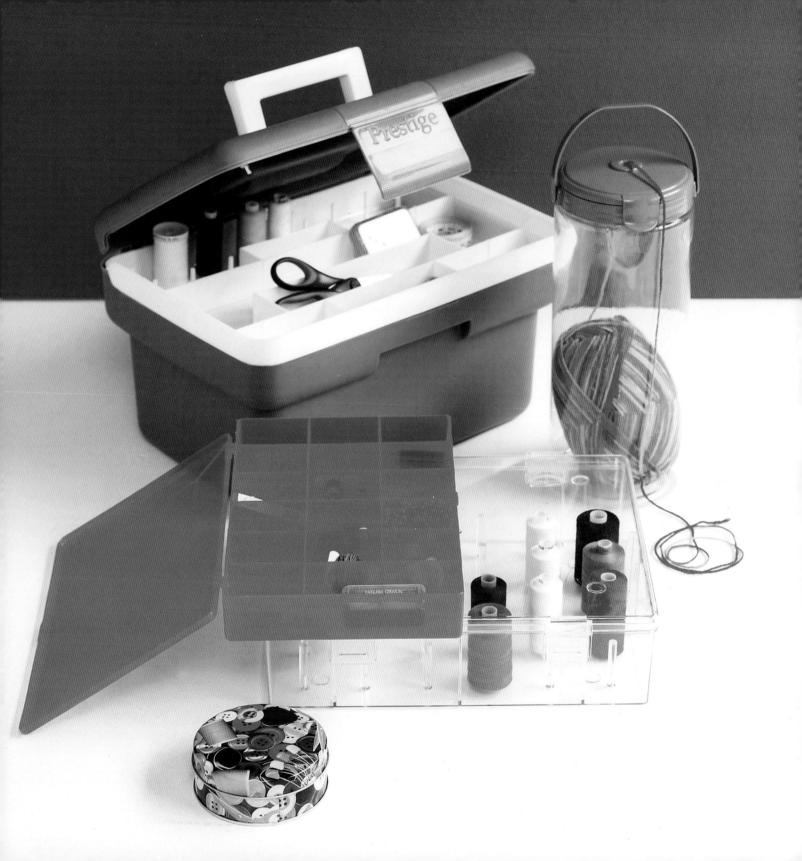

HOME HINT: *Throw away small, less usable fabric scraps and spools of thread that have just a small amount of thread left on them. They take up valuable space.*

Step 5 Once you have sorted your sewing supplies into boxes, take this opportunity to give your sewing room a thorough cleaning. These rooms can get very dusty with lots of stray threads.

Step 6 Consider whether the layout you have is the best one for your sewing activities. Would your sewing machine serve you better if placed where there is more natural lighting? Take a moment to review this and make any necessary changes.

Step 7   Once you are happy with the layout of your sewing room, turn your attention to storage options for your supplies. Perhaps you would like uniform containers to fit into a specific area or to change the size of some containers to better suit the contents.

Obviously, you need to make this consideration in conjunction with the available storage space. For example, if your sewing room is a spare bedroom, you may have a built in closet that you can use to store your supplies; if it is a much smaller space, you may only have a dedicated cupboard to store your sewing items in.

HOME HINT: *You may want to include some containers for projects that are in development. These containers should be easy to reach for when you want to continue working on the project.*

Step 8   Clearly label each storage receptacle and place it in the appropriate location.

HOME HINT: *While you are organizing your sewing room, it might be a good idea to take the time to get your sewing machine and serger serviced.*

25

HOW TO ORGANIZE MY CRAFT PROJECTS

Jeni is a crafter; she scrapbooks, crochets, knits and sews and her daughter also loves crafting. Her craft area is now so overrun with beads and patterns that spending time on her favorite hobbies is more of a chore than a joy. Jeni has dozens of project instructions, ripped-out magazine pages, other magazines with dog-eared corners, and notes or emails from friends with patterns or ideas on them that 'she'll get to one day?'

Step 1 Schedule at least an hour to complete this task. Clear some space to work in; the dining room table would be ideal.

Step 2 Gather your materials:
- A three-ring binder
- A set of at least ten tabs (get the extra wide ones)
- Clear plastic sleeves
- Scissors
- Access to a photocopier (optional)

Step 3 Gather all the craft project instructions that you have scattered around the house or office – torn out pages, emails from friends, magazines – anything you can find that has craft project instructions or ideas on it.

Step 4 Ensuring that your dining room table (or other workspace) is completely clear, start

laying out the patterns, projects, and instructions into groups. If your interests lay in multiple crafts, your categories could be:

- Scrapbooking
- Paper craft
- Crochet
- Quilting
- Beading

- Embroidery
- Needlework
- Knitting
- Sewing
- Jewelry making

If you are interested in one craft in particular, such as knitting, you could try these:

- Women's fashion
- Men's fashion
- Babywear
- Toys

- Accessories
- Children's wear
- Homewares

HOME HINT: *If the instructions are still secured in a magazine, consider photocopying it instead of ripping it out. You can then recycle the magazine by passing it on to a friend, donating it to a doctor's office or clinic, a church group, or even a playgroup (they are great for cut and paste).*

Step 5   Once you have sorted the craft project instructions into your categories, check how many duplicates you have. Do you really need three patterns for baby booties? Are they all the same? Can you perhaps get rid of one? Is there a craft project that you have tried, and it didn't work out?

Remove any that you possibly can from the collection. This is the step where you 'fine tune' the craft project instructions you have selected and make sure they are ones you are truly interested in keeping.

Step 6   Do you need to create any additional categories? For example, you might want to break down some categories even further, such as sections for Silver Jewelry, Bead Jewelry and Stone Jewelry in the Jewelry category.

HOME HINT: *What about all craft project instructions in books? You have a couple of options. (A) Photocopy your favorites and insert them into your categories; or (B) Make a note of the craft project on a piece of paper with the reference to the book and insert it into the relevant category.*

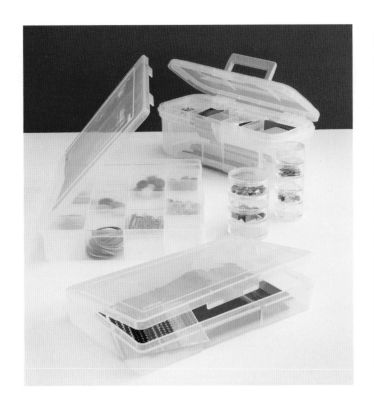

Step 7 Insert the craft project instructions back-to-back in the clear plastic sleeves and file them behind each tab accordingly.

HOME HINT: *Consider creating a second binder for filing individual crafts that you have a number of patterns or instructions for, such as jewelry:*

- *Silver jewelry*
- *Bead jewelry*
- *Stone jewelry*
- *Resin jewelry*

A great feature of this system is that each time you find a craft project instruction that you want to do, you can tear it out, photocopy or print it, and file it away immediately.

26

HOW TO ORGANIZE MY PHOTOGRAPHS

Melissa still has all her photos stored in the brightly colored envelopes from the photography store. They are in a cardboard box right beside the lovely new (empty) albums she bought to put them in… some day! She has left this project undone for so long that the mere thought of sorting and putting them into albums has all the makings of a horror movie.

Step 1 Set aside a good couple of hours for this one. I know it sounds like a long time, but organizing photos can take longer than you think. Besides, you must always allow a little time for reminiscing!

Step 2 Clear a big flat space on a dining room table or kitchen counter – not the floor. Grab some post-it notes and a pen. If you have a labeler, grab that too.

Step 3 I am going to assume the worst case scenario; your photos are in a mixed pile/box/ tub/stack that needs sorting, yes? Grab them all and bring them to the table/counter.

Step 4 Pull out the empty photo albums that you have previously bought for organizing your photos – I know you have them!

Step 5 Let's start sorting. The most difficult part is deciding where to start. Most people want their albums to be in chronological order and frustrate themselves when they pick up photos and think, "Oh, I can't remember when that was".

  You don't need to organize them chronologically. You can sort them into categories instead.

Step 6 Using your post-it notes, start writing categories for your photos. These can be holidays, birthday parties, Christmas, pets etc, but don't stop there. Think of as many categories as you can apply to your family photos.

HOME HINT: *If you can't remember dates, create an album for a person. You might create an album just for your daughter by placing all the photos of her in one album regardless of dates.*

Step 7 Take each photo and place it into the appropriate category. You may find that you have to add a few categories as you go along, but keep going! Now is not the time for stopping!

Step 8 Once finished, take each category of photos, and stack them into one single pile again. Be sure to use the yellow sticky notes as the 'dividers' between each category.

Step 9 Take the top pile and spread them out on the table / counter and arrange the photos in a rough order. Check if you have duplicates or some images that are not suitable.

HOME HINT: *What about the photos I don't like? What do I do with them? If you don't want to look at them, then it's unlikely that you will want to show them to anyone else. It is OK to throw out photos; it's the same as deleting them in the digital world.*

Step 10 Back to your empty albums, choose an album to suit your first category.

Step 11 Check the orientation of the sleeves; i.e. are they landscape or portrait. Which way will you 'read' the photo album?

Step 12 Re-arrange the images more carefully now so they suit the orientation of the album, pairing up landscape and portrait images together so the viewer is not constantly turning the album from side to side.

HOME HINT: *Before you place them in the albums, you might want to think about scanning them into digital images. You can buy scanners from stationery or electrical stores; they will even turn old fashion slides into digital images.*

Step 13 Insert the photos as arranged and write any memos beside images.

Step 14 Create a label for the title of the album, for example, 'Family Holiday 2014', and place it along the spine of the album.

HOME HINT: *Create your albums digitally. A number of online sites allow you to upload your images and create a beautiful hardback book of your latest adventure.*

Step 15 Don't worry if the album is not completely full, but if you have only used half the album, you may choose to include another, similar, event in the same album. In this example, the label might be 'Canada 2007, Europe 2009'.

Step 16 Continue working through each pile in the same way.

HOME HINT: *If you have been on a recent holiday or have had a major event, leave the photo album out on the coffee table. That way, when friends come over, they can pick it up and flip through it. After all, that's what photos are for – sharing.*

How do I organize my digital photos?

Organizing your digital photos follows essentially the same rules as above, but instead of photo albums, you can create 'folders' on your computer or external hard drive in the same way that we have created categories above.

HOME HINT: *Save your photos to multiple places. Your laptop could suddenly die one day and then, bang, all your precious photos are gone. You can save them to an external hard drive or CDs.*

BMW

27

HOW TO ORGANIZE MY COLLECTIONS

BY DOROTHY BRENINGER

Dorothy the Organizer is America's most trusted professional organizer and an expert on the Emmy-nominated hit television series Hoarders. Though Dorothy has studied hoarding for over 20 years, she is very clear on the differences between what it takes to clear out extreme clutter and what it takes to organize a collection of heirlooms, dolls, stamps, coins, glassware, LP albums or whatever it is that people want to collect.

When organizing collections, be ready to spend time making decisions, staging your collection, and preparing BEFORE you do the actual organizing. The real organizing happens (in your mind) before you ever touch your precious belongings.

Step 1 Take some time to think critically about your collection(s). Clearly state what your collection is, whether it is art, coins, dolls or comic books, and make a list if you have more than one. Only attempt to organize one collection at a time. Decide why you are collecting or keeping the collection. Is it because it has sentimental value from the past or because it has financial return for the future?

Step 2 Retrieve and gather the pieces of your collection from all their hiding places: closets, storage, garage, family member's attic, cedar chest etc. The definition of a collection is a 'group of things'. If you have a collection and truly want to get organized – complete

with an inventory and a purpose – it is optimum to bring the entire collection into one space.

If this is a collection of smaller items, such as spoons or stamps, gathering the items together can be easy. If your collection consists of old typewriters or vintage cars, it may be more difficult.

No matter how large or small the collection is, the principle is generally the same. You need to get all of the items together so you know what you have and so that you can stage it and prepare to review, eliminate, give away, sort, display, loan, store, or sell parts, or all of it.

Step 3   Review your collection and determine it's health and whether it lives up to what you envision it as. It's important to determine whether your collection is worthy enough to keep in your home or valuable enough to loan or even sell. Consider this advice to help you decide:
- If it's broken, it goes.
- If it smells, it goes.
- If it's contaminated with bugs, mold, or animal droppings, it goes.
- Ask yourself if you have a use for it at a specific point in the future (display, sell). If not, it goes.
- Are you giving it to someone on a set date in the future? If not, it goes.
- Does it have a home (display or proper storage)? If not, then either it or something else goes to give it a home.

Step 4   Decide what you want to do with your collection. Do you want to see your collection each evening, displayed behind glass in the dining room hutch? Would you get immense satisfaction from loaning your collection to a local museum or school for a period of time? Would you feel relieved to move the collection out of your home and make money selling it? Your answers will help you decide how to inventory, enjoy, view, store, preserve, or sell your collection.

Step 5   Get your collection in tiptop shape. Now that you've eliminated any odd or broken pieces from your collection, it's time to dust or clean to breathe new air into your collection. This step requires a bit of research.

Do not use cleansers or sprays on your collections without asking the professionals. Check in with an antique shop or estate auction company (or even a museum) to inquire about the proper cleaning or repair of artwork, metals, stones, cameras, watches etc.

HOME HINT: *Keep the original packaging intact if the item's resale value is part of your reason for owning the collection. Keep any notes or paperwork that could assist in telling the story of your collection, as it will enhance its value.*

Step 6   Take note of what you have – inventory it. A collection is much more than a financial or emotional investment, especially if you are looking to sell it at some point in the future. Managing a collection requires a bit of time.

If you decide you would like to inventory your collection, you can do it in a simple manner or in a more detailed and precise way. Inventory styles include 3 x 5 note cards, excel spreadsheets, photos or videos, inventory apps for your mobile phone, and more. You are more likely to complete this step if you chose the method that is

easiest for you. Seeking perfection at this step keeps many people from inventorying and finally organizing their collection. If you choose to inventory your collection, keep the process simple and enjoy seeing what you've collected.

Step 7 Sort your collection. If you have a larger collection, you may wish to sort it into sub-categories. For example, if you collect stamps, you may wish to sort the stamps according to country or into chronological order. Having your collection sorted by sub-category allows you to split the collection into sensible groups so that you can be organized at shows and exhibits. It also makes it easier to loan a group of items out to a museum, give grandchildren equal shares of your precious collection, and more.

Step 8 Evaluate the collection. Getting involved with your collection can be very exciting, regardless of whether it has any financial value or not. Some people have a collection of shells from the beach that may carry very little or no monetary value. Others may have an Elvis Presley or a Chinese vase collection. If it matters to you, you can increase your financial portfolio by getting an estimate on your valuable pieces. You can also go online to find out what they are worth. Understanding your collection's value just might assist you in deciding how much you may wish to invest in the preservation, storage, or display of your items.

HOME HINT: *Getting an evaluation can be easier than you think. Snap a picture or pictures of your collection and submit the photo(s) to an on-line auction, estate or evaluation service. Once you submit the photo and provide a brief description of your collection, they can email you back with an estimate.*

Step 9 Preserve the collection. What does it take to keep your collection looking beautiful or saleable? Whether it is for your eyes only or for the masses, it is time to determine the steps you need to take in order to keep your newly cleaned, inventoried, and organized collection in excellent condition.
- Photos: Use acid free paper/storage boxes
- Silver: Using silver items regularly helps to prevent them from tarnishing
- Stamps: Avoid using magnetic albums
- Record albums: Use white lint-less cotton gloves and handle by the edges

HOME HINT: *Jump on line and type in the sentence, "how to preserve _____," filling in the blank with the name of your collection. You will get oodles of ideas to keep your collection healthy in the years to come.*

Step 10 Store or display the collection. Storing and displaying your collection may mean the same thing. If, for example, you collect depression era dishware, you may wish to store it in your glass dining room cabinet that also serves as a display case. Sometimes, however, we are forced to make a choice about storing a collection to keep its integrity intact for resale purposes versus displaying it for personal enjoyment.

Because you have carefully gone through all the steps, including determining your collection's value, you are better able to decide whether the items require special storage, general storage, or whether they are suitable for display. What will work best for you? Air-tight bins, cloud storage, shadow boxes, racks, shelves, hooks, soft cloth bags, boxes, tissue? Once you decide, stay committed to your choice. If you are storing it for future resale, then keep it protected. If you are displaying it for your own enjoyment, then put it where you can see it, look at it, and smile.

DOROTHY THE ORGANIZER is America's Most Innovative Professional Organizer and the best-selling author of the book, *Stuff Your Face or Face Your Stuff*.

Dorothy is the expert organizer on the Emmy-nominated weekly TV series 'Hoarders'.

She also created the 'Curb The Chaos' System which helps individuals conquer their clutter (physical, emotional and body clutter) in a pleasing and fun way. She is a member and lecturer for the National Association of Professional Organizers and Institute for Challenging Disorganization. She makes appearances on the Today Show, the Dr. Phil Show, the VIEW, QVC, and PBS in addition to being featured in the Wall Street Journal, Forbes, and O Magazines. Dorothy has co-authored five organizing books, produced the award-winning documentary, 'Saving Our Parents', and she is a high-energy, sought-after national speaker who inspires her audiences to produce results and take immediate action. She is a past United States Small Business Association Award Winner and three-time recipient of the 'Most Innovative Organizer Award'. www.DorothyTheOrganizer.com

28

HOW TO ORGANIZE MY GARAGE

John had just bought the car of his dreams, but his garage was the thing of nightmares. Years of using the garage as the storage/junk room had left him with an overwhelming task. John needed to declutter and reorganize his garage to make room for his new toy!

The dreaded Garage/Shed/Man Cave, whatever you call it, can often become the black hole of 'storage'.

More often than not, the storage can become so overwhelming that there is no room for the car, and the camping gear collapses on your head every time you need to mow the lawn.

This project is done in 2 stages.

Stage 1 – Planning Ahead

Step 1 Plan a weekend or two consecutive days in which you have no other commitments.

Step 2 You may need to gather more supplies and complete the task on the second day, so make an allowance for that.

Step 3 Check the forecast ahead of time and try to plan for a sunny day.

Step 4 Start collecting newspapers for wrapping disposed sharp items.

Step 5 Start collecting jars and other lidded containers for sorting and storage.

Step 6 You have a particularly large garage/shed, consider renting a trailer or dumpster.

Stage 2 – On the Day of the Declutter

Step 1 Start early; the sooner you start, the sooner you can finish. Have a good breakfast and get cracking.

Step 2 Lay a tarp or painter's drop cloth over the driveway or lawn area nearest the garage/shed; this will be your organizing area.

Step 3 Remove everything from the shed, laying it out on the tarp area.

HOME HINT: *Start laying items out at the back of the organizing area and work your way toward the front.*

Step 4 As items are retrieved from the shed, you may be able to decide immediately if a certain item should be thrown away. Clearly make a separate pile for those items.

HOME HINT: *If you anticipate that many items are going to be thrown away, perhaps line up a trailer in advance or order a dumpster.*

Step 5 As you lay them out, start to categorize your items according to tasks. For example, all painting supplies and equipment, power tools, nails, bolts, fixtures, garden chemicals, tools and so on.

Step 6 Continue until the garage/shed is completely empty.

HOME HINT: *While you have the mower and weed-eater out, it might be a good idea to have them professionally serviced and the blades sharpened.*

Step 7 Hose down or pressure wash the inside of the garage/shed, including the walls (if suitable), to remove all the built up grit and to create a clear space to return your belongings to.

Step 8 Move through each category in your organizing area and revise the items as follows:
- Throw away any item that is clearly past its prime, such as rusty nails, glue that has gone hard, used sandpaper etc.
- Do any items require repair? Consider whether undertaking the repair is actually financially worthwhile, particularly if it requires that a professional do the repairs. Equally, do you really think you will have time to attend to the repair yourself; how long have you been going to do it already? Be honest with yourself.

Step 9   Check the blades and handles of all garden tools. To keep handles and blades in top condition, oil them using 50% mineral turpentine and 50% raw linseed oil. This will keep the timber in good condition and help prevent the blades from rusting. Squirt the oil on and rub it in with an old cloth.

HOME HINT: *Unless you are a pro, you shouldn't use a power grinding tool for sharpening blades. Buy a new mill file, 10in long for the best control. It works really well on hedge and pruning shears and even on grass clippers. If you find files confusing, read the packaging, it will tell you if it's OK for use on garden tools.*

Step 10 When dealing with sporting equipment, think critically about what you want to keep in the space. If your children are now teenagers, it's not likely that you still need their first tricycle. If you no longer swing the golf club, find someone who does. Are you really going to get the tennis racquet re-strung? Be realistic and purge the items your family has outgrown or no longer use.

Step 11 It is time to deal with the camping gear, pull it all out and double check to see that it is correctly packed and that you have all the necessary components; it is not a good feeling when you are one tent peg short. If necessary, make a list of any items that you need to purchase to ensure your equipment is ready for your next trip.

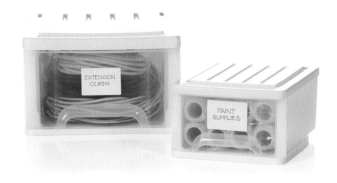

HOME HINT: *When thinking about which items to donate to charity, make sure you follow this simple rule: If you wouldn't ask a friend to pay you $5 for it, then don't donate it. Also, most charities will not accept electrical items because they need to pay to have the items tested before being able to donate or sell it. Charities don't have the funds for such expenses. Alternatively, try listing the item for sale or for free on online groups.*

Step 12 The jars and lidded containers you've been collecting come in handy for smaller items. Sort these into groups and use a black marker to label each container. Fishing tackle boxes are also a great way to keep small items organized and easy to find when needed.

Step 13 Once you have completed the review of all your items – you've decided what to throw away, containerized the small items, and taken care of your garden tools – take one last look to see if there is anything you've missed.

HOME HINT: *This process applies to anything you have in your garage. Depending upon how big your garage is, you might have BBQ and picnic supplies, suitcases, Christmas trees/decorations, and of course, a good assortment of power tools. Sort all of these into categories.*

Step 14 When returning items to your garage/shed, store the least used items toward the back and the most used ones at the front.

Step 15 Make use of wall space rather than storing things on the floor. You may already have some shelves and hooks to help you utilize the wall space. If you need more, hardware stores have inexpensive metal shelving units that are also a great way of maximizing storage spaces.

Step 16 All of this sorting and cleaning likely took up much of the first day. If you are taking a break for the evening, leave all the items where they are in the organizing area. This will give you the incentive to get back to it quickly and continue the project. After all, the stuff can't stay there forever!

Whether or not it is time to break for the evening, it is time to gather the rest of the needed supplies to organize the garage in a way that works well for your family. Take a trip to the store for the items you need to complete the project. Have a definitive list; do not offer to do other errands 'while you are out'. Go directly to the store and back home. It is too easy to get distracted.

HOME HINT: *Depending on what time of day it is when you return from your shopping, you may need to cover and secure the organizing area with a tarp and anchor it with bricks (or tent pegs) so that you can continue the next day*

Step 17 Ensure that you have created a clear path around your garage/shed that allows you to reach your storage areas/units. You don't want to be climbing over the camping equipment to reach the Christmas tree!

Step 18 Do you now have enough items in your donate or give away pile that you are considering a garage sale? Good idea, why not make some money from your efforts. Refer to Chapter 30, How to Organize My Garage/Yard Sale.

Congratulations – you now have an organized garage or shed and it is easy to access whatever you need in a flash.

You should take on this project at least once every 12 months; so put it on your calendar for next year!

29

HOW TO ORGANIZE MY GARAGE/YARD SALE

Anthony undertook a major declutter of his home and is now left with a bunch of stuff to get rid of. The idea of a garage sale was completely overwhelming for him, so I broke it down into a step-by-step process to help him get the sale organized.

Stage 1 – Preparing for the Sale

Step 1   Set a date for your garage sale about three weeks in advance.

Step 2   Start moving all the items that you think you want to sell to one central location; the garage seems like an obvious spot.

Step 3   Ask the kids if they have anything they would like to sell (encourage them by suggesting a new toy or game they could put the sale proceeds toward).

HOME HINT: *If you have a very friendly neighborhood, talk to them about your planned garage sale. They might want to contribute some of their items (and help out, of course), or it might turn into a street sale, where each house puts out a 'stall' of things to sell. This is a really successful method for hosting a garage sale.*

Step 4   Place an advertisement in your local newspaper announcing the garage sale. Make sure you highlight any products that are likely to draw shoppers. A good sample add might look like this:

'Garage Sale – everything must be sold – furniture, bric-a-brac, electrical goods, toys, all quality items... etc.'

Make sure that you include the days of the sale (i.e. Saturday 4th and Sunday 5th) and the start and closing times (i.e. 6am to 3pm).

You might want to consider including your phone number in the advert. That way, people can call you ahead of time to see if you have particular items for sale. Also, if they can't make the sale, they can still make an enquiry. Make yourself as accessible as you can to your customers.

HOME HINT: *If you are unsure how to word your advertisement, take a look at garage sale adverts in various papers and see which ones you would want to visit. Then, replicate those adverts with your own information and wording.*

Step 5   Don't limit your advertising to the newspaper. Put up flyers at your childcare center, school, church, shopping center bulletin board, and bus stops; anywhere that people can see it. The wider the advertising, the more shoppers are likely to attend.

HOME HINT: *Consider offering 'free local delivery' if you have a truck or trailer. If you can offer this service, include it in your advertisement. Again, it may attract buyers who might otherwise stay away if they don't have transport facilities.*

Step 6   Consider offering grilled sausages or hot dogs and/or coffee and donuts (make sure you include it in your advert if you plan to do this). This is a good way to attract more shoppers and raise more revenue '$1 Sausage, $1 Coffee'. It also might keep your shoppers at your garage sale just that little bit longer.

Step 7   Ask friends and family to help, even if only to keep an eye on things – shoplifting is not restricted to stores.

Step 8   Have a wet weather plan. Can you use sunshades? Can you move the sale to a patio or deck (keep security in mind)? Can you put up tarps? Or, will everything fit in the garage?

Stage 2 – Week of the Sale

Step 1 Check your local laws and community rules to see if you are allowed to set up tables on the public footpath if you intend to use that area. Some communities won't permit this.

Step 2 Have the kids make large signs to put up around the neighborhood on the day of the sale. Have them make enough to put them on the power-poles at each intersection leading to your home (take the time to count how many you will need). However, this may be against local regulations, so check first to be sure.

Step 3 Make sure you have plenty of tables; utilize fold-up tables, trestle tables, outdoor dining tables, anything you can get your hands on.

Step 4 Start setting up tables of items for sale. Make the display of items attractive and easy to view; don't have loads of items stacked on top of each other.

Step 5 Be realistic about prices and keep them in round numbers. You don't want to give things away, but remember that regardless of the amount you paid for an item, your customers will still want to buy it for less. The aim is to get rid of as much stuff as possible, so keep that in mind when you are pricing items and when people make offers.

HOME HINT: *If you have lots of small items to sell, make each table a price point. For example, "Everything on this table $10", "Everything on this table $5", and so on. This saves time individually pricing lots of small items.*

Step 6 If you can demonstrate things working, then do this; i.e. have the fridge running, the CD player going, etc.

Step 7 If you have user manuals or the original receipts for the products you are selling, make sure you have those handy. Having the original receipt can often add value to the item; however be sure to remove any ID or credit card details from the documents to ensure against identity theft.

Step 8 Have a receipt book ready (or even just a notepad and paper), just in case someone wants a receipt for their purchase.

Step 9 Gather up as many shopping bags or plastic bags as you can. Use these on the day of the sale to give to shoppers so they have something with which to carry their purchases away.

HOME HINT: *Instead of writing prices on every item, use adhesive colored dots to indicate prices. For example, 'everything with a red dot is $5'; 'everything with a blue dot is $10', and so on. Doing so can make pricing items very quick and easy.*

Step 10 Make sure you have plenty of change. If you don't have the right change, some customers will see this as an opportunity to haggle for a reduced price that matches the cash they have on hand.

Stage 3 – Day of the Sale

Step 1 Make sure that you are up bright and early. Hard-core garage sale frequenters like to be there super early. Be prepared for people to show up before your appointed start time.

Step 2 Ensure that the driveway is completely clean; you want to make it easy for shoppers to find you or the items they want to buy.

Step 3 Put up your large advert signs on the power-poles at each intersection leading to your home (as per step 2 of stage 2 above).

Step 4 Ensure that you lock your home up tight. There have been instances where homes have been robbed while everyone is out front organizing the sale and talking with customers.

Step 5 Be prepared to haggle. Again, remember that the key is to get rid of the stuff, so whatever money you make is a bonus.

Step 6   If a customer says they want an item but that they need to go to get more money or a trailer, take a deposit for the item or check the details on their driver's license. This way, they will be more likely to return to buy the item. Never let an item go without payment.

Step 7   Once the sale is over, bag up all the items that have not sold and take them to your favorite charity. Some charities will collect larger items from you. When you call them to arrange collection, they will ask what you have to donate. Keep in mind that they may not take everything you have to offer.

HOME HINT: *If you have a large number of quality items left over, hold another sale, perhaps for a couple of weeks in a row. You have already done all the hard work so, instead of taking everything back inside the house, try again!*

Step 8   Throw everything that didn't sell and that you were unable to donate away.

You now have a less cluttered home and some extra cash in your pocket to boot. Well done!

30

HOW TO ORGANIZE MY CAR

Anna has just bought a brand new car. It is used as 'mom's taxi service',
to shop for groceries, for running errands and as a mobile office for her
home business. To make sure she is giving her clients the right
'first impression' let's get the new car organized.

Step 1 Schedule two hours for this project.

Step 2 Gather supplies:
- Garbage bags
- Vacuum cleaner
- Bucket of warm soapy water
- Sponge
- Dry cloths
- Containers for sorting

Step 3 Park your car in your garage or front drive; wherever you have plenty of room to have
all the doors and trunk open at the same time.

Step 4 Set out a few basic sorting boxes or hampers, labelled 'Away' (meaning they need to
be put away in their correct home), 'Stay' (will need to stay in the car), and 'Trash'.

Step 5 Empty all the contents of the car, placing the items into the sorting bins.

HOME HINT: *Don't forget to empty your glove box and any other storage compartments in your vehicle.*

Step 6 Take out any child car seats (if you can easily refit it yourself), and ensure that the car is as empty as it can possibly be.

Step 7 Take your bucket and sponge and wipe down all the hard surfaces in the car, including the dashboard, center console, plastic floor mats and so forth.

HOME HINT: *You may want to engage a professional car detailer to give your upholstery a thorough clean and give the exterior a gleaming polish.*

Step 8 Vacuum everything, including the upholstery, the trunk etc. Get the nozzle right down in-between seats, and under and around child safety seats.

Step 9 Review the items that you want to keep in the car. Consider different storage options for the items, such as a rack in the trunk for groceries, an over-the-chair hanger for kid's toys, and so on. Put these items away in an organized fashion.

Step 10 Return all items in the 'Away' box to their rightful home.

HOME HINT: *Check the service book; is your car due for a service or just a general checkup? Now is a great time to take care of one of your biggest assets.*

Step 11 Place all garbage items in the trash.

31

HOW TO ORGANIZE MY PARTIES

Mary is the ultimate entertainer; she just loves throwing parties for any reason she can think of. She is often asked to host events for her husband's clients and associates which can add an extra layer of anxiety.

While most parties go off without a hitch, the lead up to her events can be somewhat chaotic. I need to show Mary some easy strategies for planning and executing any party!

Do you love the idea of hosting fabulous dinner parties but the notion conjures scary thoughts of hours in the kitchen, followed by sheer exhaustion, and finally, wishing you had never started. This project needs to be started 1 month in advance of your event. It is a good idea to read the entire chapter before starting.

Stage 1 – One Month Prior to the Party

Step 1   Decide on a purpose for the event. Do you intend it to be a special celebration, or just a good time to catch up with friends and family?

Step 2   Choose a date and time. This may be governed by the timing of your special event. If not, choose the date and time that suits you and don't change it unless absolutely necessary. If you are having a large gathering it is rare that everyone will be able to attend.

Step 3   Prepare a guest list. Keep in mind that there is still the possibility that everyone will be able to come, so keep your numbers realistic.

Step 4   Prepare invitations; don't forget to include an RSVP date, and to ask if they have any special dietary requirements. Provide your contact details, an email, and/or phone number.

Step 5   Send the invitations. Will they go out via the post office, through email, or will you call around? Think about the most efficient and appropriate way to convey your invitation.

HOME HINT: *You can create and send invitations and track acceptance online or, if you want something a bit more creative, some card stores offer an invitation creating service. For a personal touch, most stationery stores have gorgeous papers that you can get crafty with.*

Stage 2 – Two Weeks Prior

Step 1   Check acceptances. Follow up with anyone that hasn't responded if necessary, but only after the RSVP date has past.

Step 2   Plan your menu. Take into consideration any dietary requirements specified by your guests. You may also need to consider different food for children and adults.

Step 3   Check to see if you have enough cutlery, dinnerware, and glassware to match the numbers on your guest list and the items on your menu.

HOME HINT: *If you don't have enough matching plates and glasses, consider 'deliberately' setting your table in an un-matching manner as is common in rustic or shabby chic styles.*

Step 4   Clean your tablecloth and napkins and make sure that you have enough. You may need to purchase extras or replacements.

Step 5   Do you need to order a celebratory cake? Take the time to do so now or schedule an appropriate date to order it.

Step 6 Start shopping for something special to wear.

Stage 3 – One Week Prior

Step 1 Check acceptances; follow up with any guests that have not yet responded.

Step 2 Consider a seating plan, especially if you are making it a formal event or you are playing matchmaker! Personalized name cards can add a stylish touch.

HOME HINT: *To make place cards, get creative: make paper napkin rings that match your invitations with each guest's name on it; tie a tag with your guests name to a stem of apple or pear; use a silver or gold pen to write names on leaves from the garden; or do something equally as creative that matches your theme.*

Step 3 Order table decorations, i.e. flowers, candles.

Step 4 Make a grocery list; make sure you actually check the pantry to make sure you have the items you think you do. Shop online if time is tight.

Step 5 Choose the wine for the event. Again, consider ordering online for delivery.

Step 6 If you are preparing the meal yourself, determine whether you can make any items in advance.

Stage 4 – On the Day of the Party

Step 1 Enlist the help of your partner, room mates, or friends to do things such as set the table, make sure the wine is chilling, prepare snacks and hors d'oeuvres, or even run out for any last minute forgotten items.

Step 2 Prepare the remaining items on your menu. Aim to have as much completed as possible by two hours before party time. So, try to have everything ready by 5pm if your guests are arriving at 7pm.

Step 3 Allow an hour and a half to pamper yourself, including leaving half an hour to have a stiff drink before your guests arrive.
     On with the show!

Most of all, have fun and remember that it's not all about the food; it's about sharing quality time with friends and family.

32

HOW TO ORGANIZE MY CHRISTMAS

Joanne is mad about Christmas; it is a big event in her household and, every year, it gets bigger. To help her manage her increasing responsibilities, I created this checklist.

November

☐ Create your list of people you need to buy gifts for, any ideas you have for them, and the budget.

☐ Write your Christmas card list.

☐ Purchase appropriate number of Christmas cards or buy online from a charity.

☐ Write Christmas cards for international friends and family.

☐ Purchase gifts for international friends and family.

☐ Ship international Christmas gifts.

☐ Order the ham and/or turkey and/or seafood.

☐ Book venues for Christmas parties or Christmas day.

☐ Evaluate your Christmas decorations; do you need more or do any require replacement?

☐ Christmas lights – check the bulbs and ensure wiring is safe.

☐ Buy advent calendars for the children.

☐ Soak fruit for Christmas cake.

- [ ] Clean the oven/BBQ.
- [ ] Arrange to have the pool serviced.
- [ ] Arrange a handyman to take care of any outstanding repairs.
- [ ] Arrange to have outdoor areas cleaned and tidied.
- [ ] Arrange for house cleaning services.
- [ ] Arrange to have the carpet or furniture professionally cleaned.
- [ ] Invite guests for the holidays and/or Christmas day.
- [ ] Prepare the spare room for holiday visitors.

Three Weeks Before Christmas

- [ ] Mail Christmas cards.
- [ ] Put up the Christmas tree and house decorations.
- [ ] Put up exterior Christmas lights.
- [ ] Plan food for the holidays and prepare a grocery list.
- [ ] Start grocery shopping for pantry items.
- [ ] Buy wrapping paper, transparent tape, swing tags, ribbons and bows.
- [ ] Start gift shopping.
- [ ] Buy gifts for school teachers and/or charity gift tree at department stores.
- [ ] Check that you have enough cutlery, crockery, glassware, linen and seating if you are expecting many guests.
- [ ] Ensure your social schedule is up to date with all household members' events noted (make sure you don't have any double bookings). Arrange babysitters if necessary.

Two Weeks Before Christmas

- [ ] Wrap presents and double check that you have a gift for everyone on your list.
- [ ] Buy 'back up' gifts for any drop in visitors.
- [ ] Buy batteries for any toys that require them.
- [ ] Clean your fridge.
- [ ] Bake the Christmas cake.

- [ ] Buy gifts for staff or clients.
- [ ] Mail gifts to friends and family living in the same country as you.
- [ ] Deliver any 'local' gifts.

One Week Before Christmas

- [ ] Buy drinks and perishable foods.
- [ ] Write a time line; remember to include things such as the time required to defrost foods.
- [ ] Double check the camera battery.
- [ ] Clean the house.
- [ ] Check time of church services.
- [ ] Arrange suitable times to visit family and friends on Christmas day.

Christmas Eve

- [ ] Buy flowers for the house and table decorations.
- [ ] Wrap any remaining gifts.
- [ ] Buy any final perishable food items.
- [ ] Collect the ham, turkey, or seafood.
- [ ] Set the table (if possible).
- [ ] Gather all gifts for children's stockings.

33

HOW TO ORGANIZE MY DATE REMINDERS

At the beginning of each year, Emma is resolved to never miss her best friend's birthday or to miss sending flowers to her mother-in-law on hers. She purchases a new calendar and writes in all the relevant birth dates and special occasions... but somehow they still get missed.

Solution 1 – Manual Method

A manual method is a little 'old school' but it is a method that can be shared and seen by all at home.

Step 1 Complete a *Birthday and Special Events Annual Planner* for the entire year ahead (see page 204). It doesn't matter if is July, complete the schedule for the entire 12 months.

Step 2 Using your planner as the starting point, you will be able to see how many cards you need to purchase and your monthly budget for gifts.

Step 3 Place the planner in a prominent position, either in your kitchen, on the family bulletin board, or in the home office.

Step 4 Update your family budget to include funds for the gifts.

Step 5 Keep a copy of the planner in your gift giving area as an extra back up.

January

Name	Date	Event	Card	Gift Idea	Budget

February

Name	Date	Event	Card	Gift Idea	Budget

HOME HINT: *Place a copy of the planner in your purse so you can reference it when out shopping.*

Solution 2 – Electronic Method

Step 1   Complete the *Birthday and Special Events Annual Planner* for the entire year ahead. It doesn't matter if is July, complete the schedule for the entire 12 months. Use this planner as the starting point.

Step 2   Select your technology. It might be Outlook, Lotus Notes or an app on your Smart Phone that you use for your dates.

Step 3   Enter the dates from the planner all at once.

Step 4   The electronic method provides extra opportunities for more organization. When possible, take the time to add links to websites with appropriate gift ideas.

HOME HINT: *If you've purchased cards in advance, make sure you allocate one place in your home for cards and/or gifts. This will make it super easy when the special event arrives; card and gift will be at the ready.*

34

HOW TO ORGANIZE MY HOUSE FOR SALE

Tenayha is selling her house. She has watched all the TV shows about how to prepare your home for sale to get the best possible price, but how does she do it without an expert TV crew? In order for Tenayha to get the best possible sale price for her home, we are going to show how to organize her house for sale like a pro.

I assume that you have committed to selling and have spoken with an agent before commencing this project.

This project assumes you have already selected your agent and are preparing for your first open home or property viewing appointments.

HOME HINT: *Select your agent by referral; a personal recommendation is always best. If you don't have a referral, interview several agents and ask for references or people you can contact to ask about their experience with the agent regarding selling and buying.*

Step 1 Allow yourself plenty of time; this project may take several days.

Step 2 Gather supplies:
  • Packing boxes
  • Marker pen
  • Packing tape
  • Packing paper

Step 3 De-personalize: Remove as many personalized items as you can. This means family photos, kids' finger paintings, and so forth.

HOME HINT: *Potential purchasers want to be able to visualize themselves, not your family, in the house. Making the place neutral and less personal will make it easier for purchasers to feel at home.*

Step 4 Immediately pack these items into boxes. Label the box accordingly.

Step 5 De-clutter: Remove all excess items from the home; for example, books that are spilling out of the bookcase onto the floor, linen that has been stuffed into the cupboards, or clothes that are on the bedroom floor.

HOME HINT: *You are going to be packing to move anyway, so pack as much clutter away as humanly possible. Potential purchasers won't mind if your garage is full of neatly stacked boxes; they know you are moving.*

Step 6 Look around for anything else that doesn't belong. The aim is for the floor space and storage space to be clear, thus allowing potential purchaser to see how much space your home offers; the bigger the better. Overflowing cupboards tell the buyer that there is insufficient storage space in this home.

Step 7 De-color: You might love your bright red dining room, but chances are you are narrowing the appeal of your home with these radical inclusions. A can of paint is not a huge investment considering the potential return.

Step 8 Ensure that your newly cleared space is thoroughly clean. Nothing turns a buyer off more than dirt and clutter; it means work for them.

Step 9 Do any obvious repairs, such as unfinished handyman tasks, unpainted walls, missing or broken tiles, loose wiring and so on. You want potential purchasers to be impressed, not busy making a list of repairs they would need to complete – this could also affect the sale price.

Step 10 Review your entrance way. Is the journey from the curb to your front door appealing? Clear the pathway of weeds and dead plants.

Step 11 Mow the lawn and trim dead branches from the garden. Create a space that the new owner will enjoy.

HOME HINT: *Remove any dead plants from the garden and replace with something that is already in bloom.*

Before Viewings

Step 1 Clean, clean, clean – a home can never been too clean. A dirty home is a huge turn off for purchasers.

Step 2 Make all the beds properly. Smooth down duvet/comforter covers and plump pillows.

Step 3 Check toilet bowls for freshness.

HOME HINT: *If you don't have the right furniture to create the desired sale affect for your home, consider renting furniture for the duration of the sale campaign.*

Step 4 Straighten rugs and furniture, plump cushions.

Step 5 Pack away any stray toys or household clutter.

Step 6 Clear kitchen counter tops (no dirty dishes in the sink); put as many items from the counter tops into drawers and cabinets.

Step 7 Remove all traces of pets if they are indoor animals, take your pets with you while viewings are taking place. Someone may love your house but may be very allergic to your cat.

HOME HINT: *The bigger the WOW, the bigger the sale price!*

Step 8 Ensure that all valuable items are safely stored away and that any identifying documents are put away from prying eyes.

Step 9 Finally, ensure the house smells clean and fresh—consider adding some flowers.

Step 10 Repeat this preparation ahead of every viewing.

35

HOW TO ORGANIZE MY RELOCATION

Brothers Alex and Rick have just bought their first investment property. They are going to move from their respective rented apartments into the house for the first two years, renovate it and sell it on.

They are both excited about their first step on the property ladder, but the thought of organizing and managing all the details that are required to complete the move is overwhelming. I need to step in and help them through these easy to follow steps.

Stage 1 – Four to Six Weeks before Moving Day:

Step 1 Before booking the movers, decide which pieces of furniture you will take with you.

HOME HINT: *Measure your furniture to see if it will fit in the allocated space in the new home.*

Step 2 Once you know what you are taking, call around for quotes from various movers. They will be able to provide a more precise quote if you can be specific about the items you want to move.

HOME HINT: *Confirm that your movers will disassemble and reassemble any furniture, i.e. beds and modular sofas. If not, arrange to have this done toward the end of moving day.*

Step 3 Select your movers and book the dates.

Step 4 Start de-cluttering, now is the ideal time to part with items you no longer need. Why pay a mover to take them to a new location if you don't need them?

HOME HINT: *Start using up all opened food in your pantry and freezer.*

Step 5 Investigate schools, local utilities, and other facilities that may change with your move.

Step 6 Host a garage sale or list items online for sale that you are not taking with you. This is the perfect time to raise some extra funds to cover moving costs.

HOME HINT: *Check whether your moving company will move any dangerous chemicals that you may have on hand, such as paints, thinners, petrol fuel, methylated spirits etc.*

Step 7 Shop for packing materials; your moving company will most likely have these. Most self-storage facilities also have boxes and packing materials for sale.

Step 8 Carefully pack your belongings. Put heavy items in smaller boxes and light items in larger boxes. Check if your moving company has a maximum box weight limit. Check the removal company's insurance policy. Some will only insure the items if they pack them. Some companies may require that you take out separate insurance through your home insurance policy.

Step 9 Clearly label each box with the destination room location and its contents.

HOME HINT: *If you are leaving appliances in your home, leave behind the user's guides and any relevant warranties for the new owner.*

Stage 2 – Two to Three Weeks before Moving Day

Step 1 Set up a redirection notice at your post office.

Step 2 Advise as many authorities as possible of your new address.

Step 3 Advise all family and friends of your new address (and phone number if this is also changing).

Step 4 Return library books or anything else that has been borrowed from your current neighborhood.

Step 5 Arrange child care for your moving day if necessary.

Step 6 Organize telephone, internet, cable and gas connections.

Step 7 Plan how you will relocate your boat, motorhome or trailer.

Step 8 Book an exit clean of your current home (after you leave and before new owners or tenants move in).

HOME HINT: *If you are moving from a rental property, determine the minimum requirements of your exit, such as replacing light bulbs, cleaning the garage and so forth.*

Stage 3 – One Week before Moving Day

Step 1 Pack an 'Immediate' box of bedding to be used on the first night in your new home.

Step 2 Pack a second 'Immediate' box for items required immediately, such as medications, tea, coffee, snacks, baby needs, pet needs.

Step 3 Draw a floor plan of your new home and indicate where furniture should be placed. Give it to your movers on moving day.

Step 4 Cancel newspapers, milk or other deliveries.

Step 5   Drain lawn mower and other equipment of fuel.

Step 6   Reconfirm all services, i.e. cleaner, movers, real estate agent etc.

Stage 4 – The Day Before the Move

Step 1   Arrange the collection of keys for the new home.

Step 2   Arrange the return of keys for the current home.

Step 3   Confirm the arrival time of the moving truck.

Step 4   Have the children's bag packed for childcare.

HOME HINT: *If you have hired professional packers, ensure that they are finished the day before the truck is due to arrive.*

Step 5   Leave a welcome note for the new residents. Let them know your new address, any special instructions, when the next garage collection is due and leave all remaining sets of keys.

Stage 5 – Moving Day

At your existing home

Step 1   Once the home is empty, do a final walk through, checking every cupboard, the tops of every cupboard, under the house, in the basement, the fridge and freezer – everywhere.

Step 2   Turn the power off if instructed.

Step 3   Return keys as arranged.

Step 4   Say a final farewell to your neighbors.

At your new home

Step 5 Transport valuables and perishable items in your own vehicle.

Step 6 Be on site as the truck arrives so that you can supervise the placement of furniture and check for any damage.

Step 7 Upon arrival, check to ensure electricity, gas, phone and other connections have been made.

Step 8 Identify your two 'Immediate' boxes promptly.

Step 9 Tape a copy of the furniture layout plan in a prominent position so that everyone can reference it.

HOME HINT: *If your possessions were stored or shipped overseas, remember to triple check the inventory.*

Step 10 Once the unloading is done, check that everything is completed to your satisfaction. Double-check the condition of items. Should you find items that are damaged, immediately advise the on-site supervisor of the issue. They will be able to provide advice as to how the matter can be rectified in accordance with the company's insurance policy.

Step 11 Arrange to have the locks changed on your new home if you have any security concerns.

Step 12 Let the unpacking begin.

Step 13 Say hello to your new neighbors!

EMERGENCY PREPARATION CHECKLIST

Section 1: Emergency Survival Items:

- ☐ Water Containers
- ☐ First Aid Kit
- ☐ Torch
- ☐ Battery Opera
- ☐ Batteries
- ☐ Tinn
- ☐

36

HOW TO ORGANIZE FOR AN EMERGENCY

*If you had to leave your home with as little as five minutes' notice, what would you take? Of
course you would take family members and pets, but what else? After the event, what other
items would you wish you had taken?*

It is possible to have an emergency plan in place that would prevent confusion and stress if an
evacuation became a reality for your family? Thankfully, in the electronic and digital age we
live in, you can do plenty in advance to be prepared for such an emergency.

Photos
This is the number one item that we all want to save, especially older photos, which cannot be
replaced. Thanks to the digital age, this has now become super easy.

Here's what you can do:

Step 1 Take older (pre digital) photos that you don't have the negatives for to a photo
specialist to be scanned. You can also do this yourself if you have a decent scanner.

Step 2 If you have negatives, you can buy a scanner that will turn your negatives and slides
into digital images, these scanners are widely available at office supply stores and are
inexpensive. You can also take these to a photo specialist to be done for you.

Step 3 Digital images are the easiest to preserve; you probably already have some currently stored on your computer hard drive, right? This is OK for easy retrieval. However, I do recommend that you also have a second place to store them away from your hard drive and laptop.

Step 4 Once you have all your precious photos in digital form, you need to make a couple of backups. I recommend portable external hard drives or CDs. The reason I recommend two is that technology does have its failings and, if one of these devices should malfunction, you should have a backup.

HOME HINT: *A tip from our friend Robin, "I archive extended family photos on CDs and make several copies to give as gifts each Christmas. The family loves it, and backups are located everywhere (in every family member's house). That way, in case of fire in one location, nothing archival is truly lost."*

Step 5 Store these devices in an easily accessible location; one in your home and the second in a different location, such as your office or a safe deposit box.

HOME HINT: *Do you have any elderly family or friends who don't have access to this technology? Family history can be lost forever in a disaster. Is there anyone you can help with this?*

Important Papers/Documents/Records

These days, we all have so many things to keep track of, such as bank accounts, utilities and service providers, insurance policies, that it is nearly impossible to remember all the details. What would you do in an emergency? What about certificates, passports or awards? Could you access them quickly?

Here's what you can do:

Step 1 Keep track of your utilities and service providers by creating a very simple document that lists the name of the company, your account number, and their phone number (don't list passwords and user names in this document for obvious security reasons).

Step 2 Create a spreadsheet to list all the utilities and service providers, or if you are not into computers, you can put this information into an address book. Save this document where you saved your photos, if you use the spreadsheet option.

Step 3 When dealing with certificates, passports and awards, scan these the same way you did the photographs so that, at the very least, you will have all the details you need to order replacements. Save the scanned copies of these documents to the same location that you have stored your photos.

Step 4 If you feel comfortable with using cloud storage, you can save these documents to your Google Docs or Dropbox account.

Sentimental Objects

You may have precious pieces of heirloom jewelry or artwork that has a great deal of sentimental value.

Here's what you can do:

Step 1 Knowing where to find these items is the key. Often, I will do a de-clutter project for a client and find boxes of heirlooms that haven't been seen in over ten years.

Step 2 If you have some sentimental objects, then you should know where they are, and they should be easy to access in the event of an emergency.

Obviously, items such as jewelry, small ornaments, and small pieces of artwork are easier to take with you.

HOME HINT: *You may not be able to move furniture and larger art collections to safety on short notice in an emergency; therefore, it is critical that your insurance coverage is adequate.*

Step 3 I recommend taking photos of antique furniture and art collections that are of sentimental and monetary value and storing the pictures with your 'family' photos. As well as giving you a memento of these pieces, it will also assist with any insurance claims.

Step 4 If smaller items are of significant monetary value, it would be wise to consider a small safe in the home (see next section) or a safety deposit box at your bank.

Step 5   Ensure that all family members are aware of the location of prized possessions. If possible, they should be kept within easy access. Preferably, not down in the back garden, under the foundation of the shed.

Purchase a Small Fire Proof Box/Safe

Naturally, buying a fireproof box or safe is a good option, especially if you are in an area that is prone to bush fires. Of equal benefit, however, if the box is small and lightweight, it can be one of the items that you grab in those five minutes. You could also keep your passports in this box.

Create an Emergency Evacuation List

If you are asked to evacuate your home, panic will usually set in immediately. Our mind can often go blank at this moment and all well laid plans can disappear. The best idea is to have an easily accessible list of what to take and where to locate each item.

When the time comes to evacuate, get a laundry basket and quickly grab all the items on your list. If you have time to grab other things, only do so after you have located all of your priority items. These are the things you will need the most.

ABOUT THE AUTHOR

ORGANIZING IS WHAT ADELE BLAIR THRIVES ON

Even as a little girl, Adele's idea of a play date with a friend was to rearrange her bedroom.

Her lifelong passion for planning, sorting and streamlining was her inspiration for creating The Concierge Collective and this book.

From a very early age, Adele has been surrounded by business, with her father starting one when she was three months old. Her mother ran both the business and the family home. In this environment Adele learned first hand the importance of being organized – and how challenging that can be for busy people.

Upon leaving school, Adele attended the local college. Despite failing her Secretarial Studies, she soon landed her first position as a secretary with a government lobby group, which was a baptism of fire.

Soon after, at 19 years old, Adele moved abroad where she worked for a partner of Ernst

& Young for six years before transferring back home with the same company. In her mid-20s, Adele explored her creative side, working with top designers and architects.

Soon after marrying, Adele and her husband, Anthony, moved cities again, and she joined an international recruitment agency as a Personal Assistant. She quickly advanced in that company; first becoming their Legal Support Recruitment Consultant, and ultimately, their National Administration Manager.

Throughout her corporate career, Adele relished completing many 'outside of the box' tasks, which she happily took on even though they were outside the role of her 'normal job'. These additional tasks meant that Adele had to be extra organized to ensure that both the professional role and personal requests of her employer were managed.

Her enjoyment of, and skills in, completing such tasks prompted Adele to open her own business, The Concierge Collective, in July 2006 an endeavor that offered her the opportunity to utilize her organizational and management skills, providing an essential service that offers clients an extra pair of hands when they need it.

Building on the experience gained through the time spent with her parents' business, her further experience working in the corporate world and her own business, allowed Adele to develop the business acumen that led her to become a Finalist in the Telstra Business Women Awards, Business Owner category, in 2011.

In addition, Adele co-founded the Institute of Concierge and Lifestyle Managers. In 2014 iCALM received ASQA accreditation for the Diploma of Personal Concierge Services.

Adele is a Certified Concierge Specialise (CCS) and Accredited Expert Professional Organiser, and a Member of the National Concierge Association of the USA.

Today as well as performing her duties as Managing Director of The Concierge Collective, Adele is often asked to speak about her organizational and business expertise. When she's not working, Adele likes to travel overseas and spend time with her husband and greatest supporter, Anthony.

Learn more at:
facebook.com/howtoorganizemyeverything
twitter.com/organizehowto

First published in 2015 by New Holland Publishers Pty Ltd
London • Sydney • Auckland

The Chandlery Unit 704, 50 Westminster Bridge Road, London SE1 7QY United Kingdom
1/66 Gibbes Street Chatswood, NSW 206 Australia
5/39 Woodside Ave Northcote Auckland 0627 New Zealand

www.newhollandpublishers.com

A record of this book is held at the British Library and the National Library of Australia.

ISBN 9781742577869

Managing Director: Fiona Schultz
Publisher: Diane Ward
Project Editor: Anna Brett
Design: Andrew Quinlan
Production Director: Olga Dementiev
Printer: Toppan Leefung Printing Limited

10 9 8 7 6 5 4 3 2 1

Keep up with New Holland Publishers on Facebook
www.facebook.com/NewHollandPublishers